VITA: Adventures of a Volunteer Tax Preparer

Larry Klos

TABLE OF CONTENTS

Dedication

This book is dedicated to VITA volunteers everywhere; to those who volunteer their time to help others with confusing but important topics.

It is also dedicated to those who directly and indirectly helped me in the book's preparation. My heartfelt thanks go to my primary VITA Site Coordinator, Jeanette Hopkins, and to the other coordinators and VITA staffers who have provided the environment, endless advice, and behavior modeling examples to allow me to interact well with clients. Among that group I specifically want to acknowledge the content and editorial assistance of Michelle Pantaleo-Clough and Sue Matkin who helped greatly to finalize the document for publication.

Finally, it is also dedicated to my long suffering wife, Elaine, who was left 'abandoned' for hours and days as my attention was held by preparations for VITA certification and by months of 5 hour days providing assistance to clients in the tax office. I also wish to express my apologies to our 84 pound black Labrador, Josie, who sacrificed many walks and who whimpered unceasingly at the front window waiting for my returns. May you whimper no more (at least until next tax season). . . I think she has forgiven me.

Preface

As a retired engineering manager I had been looking for a suitable opportunity to provide volunteer support for my city and my community. I had much community and societal support through my working career; I now wanted to repay some of my social 'debts'. I have available time and skills; I wanted to find an organization where I could use that time and those skills to help others.

Although there are many worthwhile options, and nothing prevents individuals from supporting more than one option, I finally found a volunteer position which helps the community while providing me with interesting interactions and a better understanding of our world. The volunteering opportunity I found is VITA, the US Government's Internal Revenue Service (IRS) Volunteer Income Tax Assistance program.

The Volunteer Income Tax Assistance Program is an IRS initiative designed to provide free tax preparation services for low to moderate income individuals, persons with disabilities, the elderly, and those with limited English skills. Services are provided in all 50 states. The service is implemented through training and certification materials and implementation grants to local, frequently non-profit, organizations.

When I initially heard about the VITA program, it sounded good, but I was not able to find much information about how the program worked or the interactions that I would likely have with the individuals and families for whom I would be providing tax assistance. Nevertheless, I contacted the United Way of Tarrant County which sponsors and coordinates local VITA tax assistance sites. I'm glad that I did. After attending an introductory training session and receiving materials, I spent many hours reviewing the IRS developed tax preparation training and subsequently passed my IRS certification tests at the Basic and Advanced levels, as required for me to assist clients with their taxes. I made

1

arrangements with the Site Coordinator of the VITA site nearest to my home and began my first volunteer shift in late January of 2015.

That was when the fun started! The opportunity to provide services to our client base has given me a much better insight into the tax laws and the official tax forms required by the United States. It has also exposed me to some life situations of which I previously had no knowledge. Every day I have learned something new. Every day I appreciate more and more how lucky I have been in my life.

Because I could not find much information about what my tax assistance experience would be like before I volunteered, I decided to document some of my insights into the program and its clients. My hope and intent is that this book will provide prospective VITA volunteers with a good perspective of the VITA volunteer experience before they prepare for and begin their own service to the community.

The book starts with a description of the origins and operation of VITA and my experiences in the VITA 'sign up' and training process. In subsequent chapters I address the personal and financial situations of the client base that we serve and the tax laws with which we all must comply. I then cover specific examples of tax/client situations that completely surprised me; as a middle class professional I was totally unaware of some of the good and bad aspects of our tax laws and of the trying situations of many lower income families who live in our communities. Although all of the situations that I describe are taken directly from real tax returns that I have prepared, I have modified details of the situations to ensure client anonymity and privacy.

As described above, this first part of the book, Part One, is largely descriptive and factual. It provides the 'who, what, when, where, why, and how' aspects of the VITA experience. However, because I've always been interested in the sociological and societal aspects of life, I found it impossible to limit myself to these factual aspects. Much of my satisfaction with my volunteer experience derives not just from what VITA volunteers do, but rather from the insights that those activities have provided me into our tax system and how our tax system either helps or hinders individuals in their lives and helps or hinders the health of our entire society. Although I've been preparing my own taxes for my entire life, I frankly had no idea of how the taxation world worked for individuals in other financial and social situations.

Accordingly I have followed that first part of the book with a second part, Part Two, an increasingly subjective part in which I document the insights that the experience has provided to me and some suggestions for tax code improvement. I think that readers may find my comments thought provoking. Perhaps if more of us understand the involved issues and discuss possible solutions, we can influence our elected legislators to implement changes that would be good for both individuals and for our society. If some or many readers disagree with my analysis and proposed solutions, I will still be happy. I doubt that any of these ideas are unique or newly described. We need a broader understanding of our taxation approach and our social welfare infrastructure to develop a consensus approach to which we can all subscribe. We need to get more people thinking, talking, and communicating with our legislators about these subjects.

I have a few words of caution for readers. In addition to the 'Adventures' part of my VITA experience, in Part Two I provide information about the tax code, its history, and the rationale for its implementation. To the best of my knowledge this information is correct. However, this book should not be considered an authoritative reference source for tax information. If you need an authoritative reference, look elsewhere.

VITA ADVENTURES

PART ONE: VITA Adventures

Chapter One: Introduction to VITA

The Volunteer Income Tax Assistance **(VITA)** program is an IRS program designed to help lower income taxpayers complete their annual tax returns at no cost. The existing VITA Program originated with the Tax Reform Act of 1969 as part of an increased emphasis on taxpayer education programs. The VITA Program offers free tax help for low to moderate income individuals, persons with disabilities, the elderly, and those having limited English proficiency.   IRS Certified VITA volunteers prepare basic income tax returns.

The program was strengthened in 1971 through a university tie-in by an IRS agent named Gary Iskowitz at California State University-Northridge. The concept at CSU was to provide local taxpayers with free tax return preparation by accounting students, in an effort to provide both a valuable community service and a powerful hands-on learning experience for the accounting students. The program grew from a small group of dedicated accounting students to what is now a nationwide program that serves millions of taxpayers, has volunteers from all walks of life, and still provides a valuable learning experience for volunteers. Volunteers come from the local communities they serve.

Every year, beginning in December and continuing until mid-January, volunteers receive training from the IRS to help prepare tax returns in communities across the country. Volunteers are trained using classroom training, on line training materials, tax software contracted by the IRS, and accompanying certification tests to confirm volunteer competency. VITA sites are generally located at community and neighborhood centers, libraries, schools, shopping malls, and other locations convenient for low to moderate income taxpayers. Clients are not charged fees for this service. VITA sites generally assist people who make $53,000 or less (for tax year 2014) and whose tax situations are common in that demographic.

The VITA program was improved and broadened many years later, in the year 2000, by leveraging partner organizations after the reorganization of the IRS to create the Stakeholder Partnerships, Education and Communication (SPEC) function. The SPEC function structured the IRS to actively coordinate with existing community organizations to provide free tax education and preparation services with a common curriculum and level of quality.

SPEC is the outreach and education function of the IRS Wage and Investment (W&I) Division. SPEC's mission is to assist taxpayers in satisfying their tax responsibilities by building and maintaining partnerships with key stakeholders to inform, educate, assist, and communicate with customers. This approach places an emphasis on partner involvement. SPEC's partners are organizations of all types—corporate, faith-based, non-profit, educational, financial, government and military that share the same customer base. Local community partners have greater access to taxpayers, higher potential for expanded resources, and own the important intangibles of taxpayers' credibility and trust. SPEC and the local providers serve taxpayers through Tax Preparation and Tax and Financial Education. As part of education outreach, partners provide clients with information on tax issues such as the Earned Income Credit (EIC), filing responsibilities, and locations of tax assistance. They also provide clients with the information, knowledge and skills needed to evaluate their financial options and make informed financial decisions concerning saving, spending, and asset building.

VITA was further significantly strengthened in December of 2007 when Congress appropriated funds to the Internal Revenue Service (IRS) to establish and administer a matching grant program for community volunteer income tax assistance. Each year since, Congress has appropriated funding for the program. This grant funding allows partner organizations to:

• Enable the Volunteer Income Tax Assistance (VITA) Program to extend services to underserved populations in hard to reach areas, both urban and non-urban;
• Increase the capacity to file returns electronically;
• Heighten quality control;
• Enhance training of volunteers; and
• Improve the accuracy rate of returns prepared at VITA sites.

The IRS now awards grants for tax preparation in all 50 states and the District of Columbia, using volunteers with a wide variety of ages and backgrounds. The grants certainly assist local organizations, but despite the cost savings resulting from the unpaid participation of volunteers, the grants defray only a small part of the cost of running the local VITA program.

The VITA program is generally implemented jointly with the 'Tax Counseling for the Elderly' (TCE) program. The TCE program offers free tax help to individuals who are age 60 or older and is implemented through cooperative grant agreements which are entered into between IRS and eligible organizations similarly to the manner in which VITA is implemented.

Although it will not be covered further in this book, the VITA program is not the only option for people to obtain free tax help. For example, the AARP organization has a large free tax filing service, targeted to older individuals but providing broad filing services to many people. There are also many computer based free tax filing options, a number of which can be accessed through the IRS web site. Any individual who (generally) earns less than $60K per year can go to the IRS.gov web site, click on 'Free File' and find a number of different computerized online tax packages that they can use to file their taxes at no cost. Even though this income range completely includes VITA tax services, most of our clients are more comfortable coming to someone who is trained and familiar with the tax laws to get their returns done, rather than spending the effort and taking the perceived risk of doing their taxes themselves.

Chapter Two: The sign up and training process

My personal involvement with the VITA program began with a news article in the Fort Worth Star-Telegram newspaper, followed soon after by an item about VITA on the City of Fort Worth Web Page, which led me to contact the United Way of Tarrant County (which funds VITA services in our area). Through the United Way VITA Volunteer Coordinator, I was provided with a VITA volunteer packet containing information and web links to related materials and I was informed about VITA training sites, VITA tax preparation sites and the training process. I was also asked to attend an 8 hour training session in January as part of my preparation to serve as a tax preparer.

Through that information I discovered that the City of Fort Worth is partnering with the United Way of Tarrant County to offer free income tax assistance for local families through the VITA (Volunteer Income Tax Assistance) program.

All VITA volunteers are IRS-certified in tax law and must receive a score of 80 percent or higher to achieve this certification. Volunteers are also required to complete ethics training and sign the Volunteer Standards of Conduct agreements, so customers can feel confident knowing that their income tax needs are being met by high-quality, ethical professionals.

During 2015, local VITA sites processed 7,033 returns. The filers of those returns obtained $11,477,045 in refunds, including $5,164,314 from Earned Income Tax Credits. Those refunds had a huge impact on the disposable income available to North Texas individuals and families, and accordingly on the local economy of Tarrant County. From a tax preparation cost perspective, assuming an average cost of $300 per tax return if our filers had used a commercial tax preparer, our local VITA filers collectively saved over $2.1 million dollars in tax preparation costs alone.

This year (2015) VITA Free Tax Center sites were located across Tarrant County, including the Tarrant County College Opportunity Center, the south campus of Tarrant County College, Opening Doors for Women In Need, Community Enrichment Center, Southside Community Center, GRACE in Grapevine, Catholic Charities, the Northside Community Center, and several sites in Arlington.

The Fort Worth VITA program sought volunteers from June through January to assist during the tax filing season, from late January to April 2015. Volunteers were solicited for the following positions:

- Greeters, who welcome and direct customers while overseeing sign-in.

- Intake specialists, who ensure customers have the necessary documentation to complete their income tax return and help them complete the information in their VITA packet.

- Interpreters, who provide free interpretation and translation services to customers not fluent in English, or customers who need additional assistance.

- Tax preparers, who prepare tax returns and discuss the return with the customer after a quality review process is complete.

Prior to the January training sessions, I reviewed the materials and completed the Volunteer Standards of Conduct training. The six Standards Of Conduct to which all volunteers are required to agree are:

1. Follow the Quality Site Requirements (QSR).

2. Not accept payment or solicit donations for federal or state tax return preparation.

3. Not solicit business from taxpayers you assist or use the knowledge you gained (their information) about them for any direct or indirect personal benefit.

4. Not knowingly prepare false returns.

5. Not engage in criminal, infamous, dishonest, notoriously disgraceful conduct, or any other conduct deemed to have a negative effect on the VITA/TCE Programs.

6. Treat all taxpayers in a professional, courteous, and respectful manner

During the January training session all of the students were given hundreds of pages of hard copy training materials as well as a 232 page, spiral bound, IRS publication 4012 'VITA/TCE Volunteer Resource Guide' for 2014 returns. (TCE stands for Tax Counseling for the Elderly). We were also given a web link for IRS VITA/TCE Central, which provides extensive on-line information including:

- Link & Learn Tax lessons, which are self-paced e-learning, tax software assisted, VITA training. The training covers the return preparation process and applicable tax law.

- Certification Tests at the Basic, Advanced, Health Savings Account, Cancellation of Debt, and Military Levels,

- Volunteer Standards of Conduct training and certification.

- Practice Problems

- Electronic Copies of the Training Guides

Before I started the VITA training I was of the belief that it would not be very difficult. I have a Bachelor's Degree in Physics, I worked for over 40 years in a technical engineering field in the aerospace industry, and I am intelligent. Further, I've been preparing my own taxes, both manually and with tax software support for more than 40 years. With my background, how difficult could it be to pass the IRS test?

The answer was that for me it was hard! It was non-trivial and took me a long time to review and understand all of the materials. I was surprised and challenged. I started in November and studied in my spare time through the Christmas and New Year's holidays, finally passing both the (open book) Basic and Advanced certification levels. After thinking about my situation, I finally realized that there were several reasons why it was unexpectedly difficult for me.

- Tax laws are more complex and convoluted than they were 40 years ago. It seems that it gets worse every year. Partial confirmation of this is that the spiral bound IRS publication 4012 Volunteer Resource Guide is 232 pages long, and includes 17 major sections.

- As a salaried professional with an upper middle income background, I had no prior experience with the Earned Income Credit and other rules which are focused on people with lower incomes.

- As I've been getting closer to 70 years old, I've begun to realize that my short term memory isn't as good as it was formerly, so even after I learn (or relearn) something, it is harder to remember where to make entries and the rules that must be applied.

- My VITA training instructor said that she had a larger class than expected. Further, the room wasn't configured with the projection equipment needed for good instruction. Although each of the students had their own computer, the instructor's computer did not have the ability to project the instructor's computer screen so she had no way to easily keep the class together or to visually share the specifics of the training that she was providing.

- Although I got 90% on the open book tests, I was and am concerned that prepared tax returns should be 100% right, not the 80% required to pass the test. When actually helping people with taxes, this issue is ameliorated because each VITA site operates under the leadership of an experienced and certified Site Coordinator who is available for questions and to provide clarification. Further, the coordinator (and/or another trained and certified individual) always does a quality check on drafted tax returns, per VITA standards, before finalization.

After my training and successful certification at the Basic and Advanced levels I began to serve at the Opening Doors for Women in Need site in the Como neighborhood of Fort Worth. Although the United Way VITA coordinator said that there were tax preparation openings at many sites, I picked the Opening Doors site because it is less than a 10 minute drive from my house. When faced with a number of choices of locations at which to serve, I defaulted to the most convenient option. When taking the certification tests, I used the 'open book' provisions of the tests liberally to ensure that my answers to test questions and my preparation of example tax returns followed tax laws. Although I was initially skeptical about whether open book tests were appropriate, I am now fully supportive of that approach because of the complexity of tax law and because the information in our Publication 4012 Resource Guide (and via web access to all IRS tax publications) is available to tax preparers as they complete actual returns for real clients. If in doubt, I check it out.

Chapter Three: General Tax Observations

Although my primary motivation for joining the VITA program was to help others, I have found the experience to be personally very rewarding and educational. I have always believed that I am open minded and respectful in my treatment of others, but I am discovering that there is a whole grouping of life situations of which I have been largely unaware. My VITA experiences are helping me to grow as an individual at the same time that I am helping others. Before diving into specific cases and examples of VITA activity, I want to share some general observations. These observations fall into several groupings, those groupings are:

A. The Taxpayer Experience,
B. Comments about our VITA clients and my experiences as a VITA volunteer,
C. Comments about the challenges and lives of typical VITA clients, and
D. Comments about common tax filing approaches and strategies that I see frequently.

The typical VITA client faces many tax provisions that affect their lives, provisions with sometimes obscure and difficult qualifications. As VITA volunteers we have an obligation to help our clients take advantage of the provisions of the tax code that affect them. The VITA training makes clear that we, as volunteers, are not liable for innocent mistakes that we make in tax preparation or for preparing client returns which include fraudulent information, as long as we do not include information that we know is false or file returns that we know are fraudulent. The taxpayer signs the returns. The taxpayer is responsible for the truth of their returns.

A: The Taxpayer Experience:

When clients arrive they are asked sign in, to fill out a standardized three page intake/interview form, and to sign privacy releases. The releases are solicited to provide United

Way and Partner agencies with information about the client base and to use that information to help them align social services with client needs. Clients are provided with a list of United Way Affiliated Agency Services in which they might have interest. Our United Way of Tarrant County provides or coordinates services in four general areas: Getting a Better Education, Improving Personal Finances, Getting a Better Career or Job, as well as Taxpayer Assistance. The United Way promotes such long term benefits for our clients in many ways, including a 30/40/30 program suggesting that clients aspire to use 30% of any tax refund to pay debts, 40% to have fun, and 30% to save or invest. In the Tarrant County area printed information on available programs is provided in both English and Spanish. A language translation service telephone line can provide assistance in many other languages if needed.

VITA has sites in various locations around the county. I volunteered on the west side of the city at the Opening Doors For Women in Need (ODWIN) site on Horne Street in the Como Neighborhood. At ODWIN we helped clients in the order in which they arrived. During peak periods we frequently put extra chairs in the narrow but long hallway which was filled with people waiting to have their tax returns prepared. While waiting, their laps were full of their tax papers, purses, jackets, cell phones, and sometimes the odd child, as they used clipboards to fill out intake forms which listed important information about their tax situation. The intake forms request the information needed to file taxes, including names of taxpayers and dependents, Social Security numbers, types of income received, types of expenses paid, and life events experienced by the taxpayers during the tax year. To make life a little more bearable while they waited, our site also had small bottles of water that we gave to those who were thirsty. On more than one occasion we have also given waiting clients small bags of chips and other snacks, and I once gave a client my own personal snack. We like to prevent people from fainting from hunger or thirst in the lobby while they are waiting.

B: Comments about VITA Clients and my Experience as a Tax Preparer Volunteer:

I mentioned earlier that our certification examinations, which confirm that we are qualified to serve as tax preparers, are 'open book' exams. Through the VITA program the IRS provides each tax preparer with the Publication 4012 Volunteer Resource Guide. When doing returns I actively use that book as it was intended to be used. My 4012 document is getting well-thumbed and a bit grey around the edges. Further, I have stored electronic versions of the 4012 and several other tax documents on my laptop to support word searches if I need additional confirmation, clarification, or guidance while preparing a return. (Anyone, but especially potential volunteers, can access any of the publications mentioned in this book though the IRS website, irs.gov.)

Although I have all of this material on hand and readily accessible during tax preparation, I have discovered that the availability of such resource materials does not substitute in actual practice for experience and a good memory. The problem when actually doing tax prep for people is that we generally have a waiting list of people wanting tax help and we don't have much time to prepare returns. If our clients have already been waiting for 20 minutes in the lobby, I don't want to make them wait more during my entry of their tax data into the computer because I need to pause to research specific points of tax law. Although I spend the time needed for each return, I simply don't have time to search through all of the reference materials to puzzle out the answer to unusual questions about how the tax forms should be completed. Luckily (and by plan) the VITA program has a solution to this problem, which is the availability of the Site Coordinator. Typically, unless I am between clients, I only go to my 4012 Resource Guide if I know I can quickly find the answers I need. If my question is difficult, I let the Site

Coordinator know I need help and I move on to another portion of the return. Invariably my Site Coordinator has addressed the difficult issues allowing me to complete returns expeditiously so as to allow the taxpayers to leave soon with a correctly prepared return. Each time it happens I get more experience and am less likely to need to ask the same question again.

Many, perhaps most, of our clients are return customers from prior years. We provide a valuable service, both in preparation of taxes and in informing our clients of other United Way coordinated services which might be to their benefit. Since commercial preparers charge clients hundreds of dollars for return preparation and since many of our clients are already limited in financial resources, our services are much appreciated. Although I've never been good at remembering names and faces, Jeanette Hopkins, the Site Coordinator at ODWIN, has a phenomenal ability to remember prior year clients and welcome them in a friendly way. She also unfailingly thanks them for coming to our site for tax preparation and expresses to them her hope that they will return the next year . . . and many do return year after year. As with any client service organization, if you are nice and respectful to people they will be nice to you, and will return.

Our VITA site opened for service to the public this year on Tuesday, January 20, 2015. I had expected that the first several weeks of tax preparation would be light weeks. After all, businesses are not required to get their W2s, 1099s, etc. out until the end of January and taxes are not required to be submitted to the IRS until April 15th. I was looking forward to having a few slow weeks to build up my skills and do some additional studying about some nuances in tax preparation. I was rudely surprised because our waiting room had nearly wall to wall people for the first month we were open. For me it was a baptism of fire, I had only rare quiet periods between clients. When I commented about my surprise, my Site Coordinator said that there is always a rush of tax preparation in late January and early February. Apparently this is due to the Earned Income Credit (EIC) and child tax credit provisions which provide many working people with refunds; many with much larger refunds than the amount of taxes that they paid during the year. (I provide more information about the EIC and Child Tax Credit in the next chapter). Knowing now about the EIC I'm not surprised that people file as early as they can. When someone may be barely making it financially, getting a big refundable credit from the IRS helps a great deal. The sooner the better.

C: Comments about the challenges and lives of typical VITA clients.

Most of our clients have very low incomes, many much below the 2014 tax year's $53,000 maximum income threshold for VITA services. I think about half of clients that I've had so far have made less than $10,000 a year and many of these are supporting themselves and one or more dependents on that income. My clients generally take the Standard Deduction because they don't have enough itemizable expenses to benefit from itemization. It was amazing to me that people can survive and support families on incomes of less than $10,000 a year. Apparently they have some survival strategies which I lack. I'd love to know those survival strategies (but not badly enough to want to share their circumstances and learn through personal experience).

Most clients get refunds and most have their refunds provided by direct deposit to their bank accounts, partly because refunds obtained in that manner are paid to them by the IRS within 10 – 14 days. Although most people have their refunds provided by direct deposit, I was surprised that many appear not to have checking or savings accounts. They don't carry checks with them and instead provide the needed routing and account numbers on a piece of paper. This puzzled me until I realized that many people have prepaid debit accounts which act like checking accounts and may be provided by employers for direct deposit of pay. They can

also be obtained by taxpayers directly from the financial institutions that provide them. In researching these types of cards, I discovered that they can be obtained without providing payment history and without personal credit checks and are safer than usage of checks or cash. In addition to being easier to obtain, apparently there is also a culture issue as some individuals are leery of banks and prefer to have their pay immediately deposited by their employers into their debit card accounts (which also saves the workers check cashing fees). Additionally I've been told that some immigrants have had bad experiences with banks in their home countries and prefer not to use banks, instead they operate on a cash basis or an 'unbanked' basis using debit cards.

Given that many clients do not have savings accounts perhaps because they generally don't have any money t save, there appears not to be much of a culture of period and regular savings. In order to foster financial planning a savings, the IRS permits tax refunds to be received throu mailed checks, by direct deposit to bank accounts, or issuance of US Series I Savings Bonds. As a part of the Un Way 30/40/30 program (discussed a few pages ago), clients as we are finishing their returns if they would li receive part of (any) refund in US Savings Bonds. Gen this offer is received with blank looks. Our general clien seems not to be aware of what Savings Bonds are, th term savings objectives that they could satisfy, the f Series I bonds are inflation protected, or that bonds be issued directly in the name of a child or other dep The most extreme response to my offer of savings b a response to the effect of "Why would I want to p in Savings Bonds?" Although I don't have statistic support my conclusion, it seems to me that m clients have not been informed of opportunities and are living in a local culture which does n resources or inclination to obtain the benefits savings associated with long term planning. Al'

facts are discouraging, I realize that it will take time, years, to grow a culture which recognizes the benefits of saving 'for a rainy day'.

After all of their income is entered and the IRS Standard Deduction and Exemptions are subtracted, a large majority of clients are left with no (zero) taxable income. Since most of our clients also get refundable Earned Income Credits and many get Child Tax Credits, typical tax refunds for clients with no taxable income range from $1,000 to $6,000.

Many of our clients are unmarried and have children, dependent parents, or other qualifying dependents and as such are entitled to file as 'Head of Household'. The Head of Household status affords an increase of the Standard Deduction (in 2014) from $6200 to $9100. Although not always beneficial if their taxable income is too low, the Head of Household designation accurately reflects their role as majority breadwinner in their home and the fact that they pay more than half of the expenses for their families.

The Racial/Ethnic balance of clients who have requested tax help at the Como site is fairly evenly split between Black and Hispanic with a reasonable number of Anglos and other racial minorities thrown in as well. The age range of clients spans the age of working and retired people, from young people barely starting in the working world and paying taxes for the first time to senior citizens who have been in the workforce for years but are now significantly supported by Social Security and income from retirement, savings, and disability plans. The education range of our clients varies widely, from elementary school only to completion of college. Many of our clients are not very experienced with tax policies and rules. Others have already reviewed their tax situations with commercially available tax software packages but prefer to have a trained person formally enter and electronically submit their tax forms.

Uniformly and without exception all of the clients that I have assisted have been friendly and pleasant, even during

times when I've had to ask the Site Coordinator for assistance or clarification. They have all been appreciative of the time that VITA volunteers spend to assist them with their returns and many have expressed their thanks because we provide this service without compensation.

D: Comments about common tax filing approaches and strategies that I see frequently.

Sometimes it is obvious and sometimes less so, but we periodically have taxpayers who come in to get their returns done, but then leave without finishing the return or having us file it electronically. While most of these individuals come back to complete their returns I've been told by some of the VITA Site Coordinators that some individuals 'tax shop' to see which tax service will provide them with the biggest refund or lowest tax payment. Although all tax preparers, from whichever site, should reach the same conclusions about taxes and refunds owed, I'm sure that some preparers inadvertently fill things out differently and get different answers. It just happens. All we, as VITA tax preparers, can do is to be gracious and let them go their way. We are here to help; whether individuals want to take advantage of our help is up to them. On the flip side of this discussion we have had a significant number of taxpayers who have started out at a paid tax preparation firm, only to come to us when they find out how much they will be charged. In at least one case the local commercial tax firm actually recommended that the client who wouldn't or couldn't pay come to our VITA site.

As a VITA volunteer, we all need to be prepared for the periodic normal facility problems that happen to any house or business. At various times during my VITA service I experienced power outages, internet outages, VITA server failures, rooms that were too hot or too cold, stopped up toilets and the occasional gun battle in the street outside. Things will happen; they do happen; we need to learn to live with it. While frustrating, many of these situations were also

21

funny in retrospect and are covered in more detail in Chapter Five.

It is not unusual for people to arrive with missing W2s or other tax forms. We've been able to get some of the information on line or by telephone while preparing the returns, but in most cases the individuals need to go home, collect or obtain the needed information, and return on another day. We've recommended to several clients that they go downtown to the federal building and ask the IRS office for tax transcripts. Another variant of this situation is when people bring us any and all of their information which could possibly be tax related in the expectation that we will sort it out for them. Sometimes we help; other times we send them home to get organized. Our decision about whether to help is informal and depends on the number of volunteers for the day, whether anyone else is waiting, and the degree of disorganization of the materials. In one extreme case an individual brought in an approximately 8 inch stack of paperwork, with many envelopes not even opened. The VITA Intake volunteer for that day spent considerable time with the client sorting through the paperwork, pulling the 'tear strips' off of W2s, and preparing the information for entry into our TaxWise software program. We help if we can while being fair to others waiting in the lobby.

Since 2014 was the first tax year where health coverage was required, we had a number of people who didn't know how to respond when we asked them if they have Minimum Essential Coverage (MEC) as required by the Affordable Care Act (ACA). If they were unaware or only marginally aware of the program, how could they be expected to know? A number indicated that they had limited coverage health plans and we had to inform them that limited plans in general are not MEC and that they would have to pay a penalty unless they qualified for an exemption. We've filed many exemptions of multiple kinds, although the most prevalent exemption is because their income is below the tax filing threshold, which simply requires us to fill out entries on a couple of forms. In cases like this I always spend extra time telling them that the penalty will increase in coming years and letting them know about potential insurance subsidies and how they can find out more information. While I have never had a client who expressed happiness about penalties, at least they didn't blame us at the tax office for the problem.

We have helped a number of taxpayers who would be getting refunds on their taxes, but who owe the IRS money on prior year returns. In cases like this, the IRS will take portions of their refund as necessary to satisfy their arrears and only after those debts are paid provide refunds to the taxpayer. There are hardship exceptions to this rule and we inform the taxpayers how to contact the IRS to see if they qualify. (Later chapters will provide more information about the ACA and exemptions.) Similarly we've had a number of clients who owe taxes associated with their return and, while not disputing their obligation, say that they don't have the ability to make the payments. We always tell such clients to contact the IRS, make their case, and see if they can establish a payment plan or other arrangement to address their tax debt.

Within the limits of our time during tax season, we will prepare prior year tax returns for our clients. Two VITA Free Tax Center sites are also open all year to assist clients with prior year tax returns and other tax support.

Many taxpayers have questions about dependents. Our IRS Publication 4012 has many pages of information that provide guidance on when an individual can be claimed as a dependent so the client can benefit from the dependent's exemption and potentially other tax provisions such as 'Head of Household'.

Frequently taxpayer's taxable income zeros out, that is, they don't owe any taxes because their deductions and exemptions are greater than their Adjusted Gross Income (AGI). Taxpayers may have low income for many reasons, including low wage jobs, unemployment, retirement with most income being non-taxable Social Security payments, or large tax families relative to income. Low income levels can ease our work because if income is that low it will not matter whether the client can itemize and it also may not matter whether they file as single or head of household.

The Earned Income Credit is a major tax provision for many VITA clients. Although the larger credit amounts occur for families with dependent children, EIC is also paid at much lower levels for adults without dependents. It is not unusual for unmarried parents (thus not filing jointly) to split their children for tax purposes. I have seen all combinations of approaches, such as parents alternating years for declaring their children as dependents, or parents with multiple children deciding who takes which child in any given year.

I said earlier that very few VITA clients itemize their deductions. They don't itemize frequently for several reasons. One common reason is because, with their limited income, they are more likely to rent housing rather than own their own home and thus they have no mortgage interest payments or home property taxes to deduct. Additionally, with their limited income, they are less likely to make large charitable contributions and for both reasons combined they generally are money ahead to take the Standard Deduction.

Chapter Four: Important Tax Codes

There are some aspects of the tax code and tax return preparation process which also deserve general comments because they flavor the interactions that we have with our clients. Because the current tax system in the United States has evolved over many years and in accord with many unique laws, frequently with differing objectives, the code can appear at times to be inconsistent and even somewhat arbitrary. As a person who is intrigued by sociology and the impact that government laws have on people, I have found these topics interesting, as well as puzzling, and have enjoyed trying to figure out how the tax systems works and why the tax laws exist as they do. As a VITA volunteer, I have also found that a general understanding of some key parts of the tax code can allow me to provide better and faster tax preparation service to our clients.

In terms of impact on our client community the most important or least understood tax code topics are:

1) The Affordable Care Act
2) Tax Deductions and Refundability of Tax Credits
3) Head of Household Filing Status
4) Earned Income Credit and Child Tax Credit
5) Non-Employee Compensation and
6) Tax rules associated with citizenship.

Each of these topics addresses tax rules related to social programs. Although I cover additional history and technical details of some of the associated programs in a future chapter, I am introducing these six topics in the paragraphs which follow because of their impact on the VITA client base.

 Although the preparation of tax returns for our clients is our primary VITA responsibility, we also need to ask our clients questions that elicit information needed to prepare their tax returns correctly. We cannot expect our typical clients to understand the details of the tax code and conditions under which tax rules are, or are not, relevant. In the following sections I highlight some of the areas which are frequently misunderstood or troublesome.

The Affordable Care Act (ACA) requires most Americans to obtain health insurance which provides Minimum Essential Coverage (MEC). For people of limited means it also provides subsidies to make insurance through health care marketplaces affordable. For the 2014 tax year the ACA (also informally known as Obamacare), is causing some problems because this is the first year when penalties are charged if people do not have healthcare coverage (or an exemption from that health coverage mandate). I have found that the children of many of my clients are covered by Medicaid. The parents themselves only infrequently have insurance. When they don't, they either pay the minimum $95 penalty (or one percent of income) per adult or qualify for one of many exemptions, including exemptions for having an income so low that insurance is not affordable. Although the formal ACA Marketplace issues exemptions and documents both the coverage and exemptions on form 1095-A which is sent to the taxpayer, we've seen very few of those forms. Most exemptions that we obtain for our clients occur because taxpayer income is below the filing threshold and we can simply fill out a Form 8965 to confirm an exemption is appropriate. Despite extensive media coverage, many people are still not aware that they may be able to get subsidized health coverage and will need to pay penalties if they don't obtain that coverage. Individuals are encouraged to obtain coverage through their employer, through the private insurance market, or failing that through the ACA Marketplace. As tax preparers it is easy for us to confirm Marketplace health coverage because such coverage for taxpayers is documented on Form 1095-A. It is more difficult to determine whether taxpayers have employer or privately obtained coverage which meets Minimum Essential Coverage (MEC) requirements. We ask probing questions about coverage and, unless we independently know more facts, we accept taxpayer assertions about their MEC coverage. (For

26

tax year 2015, MEC coverage of other kinds will be documented on forms 1095-B and 1095-C).

The fact that the ACA requirement was generally not understood by most of the clients that we served for 2014 returns will also potentially impact the 2015 returns that they will file in early 2016. It may be worse because, while taxes are not required to be filed until April 15th, the 2015 open enrollment period ended on Feb 15th, two months earlier. Accordingly many clients did not find out about the insurance penalty until it was already too late for them to enroll for 2015. On about Feb 20th the US Government realized the problem and announced a special enrollment period for individuals who did not know about ACA penalties, with the special enrollment period starting March 15th and ending April 30th, for the 2015 year only. If tax payers who first found out about the penalty during preparation of their 2014 taxes took appropriate action, they may be able to avoid a more expensive penalty when they file their 2015 taxes.

Next year and in following years the problem for uninsured individuals is going to be much worse, because the minimum penalty goes up from $95 to $325 and then in the next year to $650 per individual. VITA volunteers will need better training on ACA coverage and exemptions in future tax years. In accordance with current ACA plans, at least the job of VITA volunteers will be made easier for 2015 and subsequent tax years because employer plan coverage and private insurance providers are required to document MEC insurance options to their employees and clients using Forms 1095-B and 1095-C. Many of the exemptions that can be claimed at tax preparation time seem complex and it is difficult to quickly determine whether clients qualify. Advance payment of subsidies for those who obtained subsidies is also causing some problems because advance payments can be made directly to insurance companies and if the taxpayer's income goes up or down significantly during the year, the subsidy will be recalculated and people either get a larger refund or have to make payments to compensate for inappropriately large subsidies. This can be painful at tax time. Because the yearly income of many VITA clients is unpredictable, going up or down depending on the vagaries of the short term employment market, it is frequently not possible for them to correctly forecast proper subsidy levels. Although there is a Form 8962 used at tax time to assist with calculation of what the subsidies should have been, even those calculations are somewhat difficult to use for VITA tax volunteers.

Moving to the next topic in this chapter, there are differences in the tax code between **tax deductions and refundability of tax credits**. A Tax Deduction reduces taxable income and is related to a person's marginal tax bracket — for example, if a person is in the 20% tax bracket, a $500 tax deduction will save them $100 in taxes. A tax credit, in contrast, reduces their tax liability dollar-for-dollar. This means that a $500 tax credit may take $500 off their tax balance due. Every taxpayer can take advantage of tax deductions and may or may not be able to use tax credits.

However, not all tax credits are created equal. Most tax credits are nonrefundable, which means that any excess amount expires the year in which it was available. A nonrefundable credit is subtracted from income tax liability, up to the total amount owed. A nonrefundable credit cannot reduce the tax balance below zero. The child tax credit is an example of a non-refundable credit.

Some tax credits, however, are refundable and can actually increase tax refunds. Refundable credits are treated just like the tax payments that a person makes to the IRS, such as income taxes withheld from paychecks. A refundable credit is subtracted from the amount of taxes owed, similar to the way the tax withheld from paychecks is subtracted from total yearly tax liability. A refundable tax credit <u>can</u> reduce tax liability to below zero. Restated, if the amount of a refundable tax credit is more than the amount of taxes due, the difference will be given back to the tax payer as a tax refund. If a person is already owed a tax refund, the refundable credit will be added to increase the amount of the refund. The Earned Income Credits is an example of a refundable credit.

Taxpayer Filing Status is an important issue for the VITA taxpaying client base. Single individuals with dependents can be eligible to be classified as '**Head of Household'**, which has an improved Standard Deduction (from $6200 to $9100 for 2014) and thus has a potential for tax savings. Although the rules for when a taxpayer can qualify as a Head of Household are explicit, it is sometimes difficult for taxpayers to determine whether they meet the requirement that they provide more than half of the cost of keeping up their home.

Costs that can be counted include rent, repairs, home taxes, food, etc. However, Temporary Assistance for Needy Families (TANF) funds or other public assistance funds that the client receives are counted as part of the total cost of keeping up the home, but are not counted as part of the taxpayers share when determining whether the clients pay more than half of the costs. Somewhat obviously, only one person living in the same dwelling can file as Head of Household, since mathematically only one filer could be paying more than half of the costs.

My Site Coordinator said that the IRS monitors Head of Household filings by address and that returns have been rejected when more than one person at the same address attempts to file as Head of Household.

Even though the request for information about the taxpayer's filing status appears early in the client's information sheet and on IRS form 1040, I have learned to expedite my tax return completions by delaying probing questions about filing status until I have entered all of the client's income and dependent information. I delay because if the client's adjusted gross income is less than their combined deductions and exemptions as a single person, their taxable income will be zero and any added amount in their standard deduction due to Head of Household status will make no difference to their taxes owed or to their refund received. In this case I simply inform them of the rules that would qualify them for Head of Household status, tell them that filing as Head of Household will make no difference in their situation and enter the filing status with which they respond. If filing status <u>will</u> make a difference, I go into more of the details of the rules that qualify them as Head of Household to make sure that they could support their selection as Head of Household and then (as before) enter the filing status with which they respond. As always, the taxpayer is liable for the correctness of their returns; we have an obligation to make sure that they make informed decisions when there are choices such as Head of Household filing status.

Earned Income Credit (EIC) Benefits greatly affect the tax obligation for many individuals in our client base.   The history of the Earned Income Credit (EIC) and the Child Tax Credit (CTC) are described more fully in Chapter 6. Simply put however, the EIC program provides a lower tax burden or a tax refund for those taxpayers who are working to support their families. The EIC is the largest government assistance program for low income working families. At lower income levels, the EIC benefit increases with the number of dependent children and also increases with the amount of earned income. After earned income gets higher the amount of EIC benefit begins to decrease until it disappears altogether. Particularly for lower wage earners with children, the EIC and the CTC have a dramatic effect on tax obligations and/or refunds.   Calculation of the benefit is somewhat complex because EIC and CTC have differing eligibility rules and because the phase-out income levels of these programs differ. Although not discussed here because its usage is less prevalent for VITA clients, a third dependent oriented credit (Credit for Child and Dependent Care Expenses) also has different rules.

The Child Tax Credit is a non-refundable tax credit that may reduce taxes by as much as $1,000 for each qualifying child. The 'Additional Child Tax Credit' is a refundable credit for which taxpayers may be eligible if they are not able to claim the full amount of the Child Tax Credit because their income is too low relative to their deductions and exemptions.

Filers can only claim a child tax credit or additional child tax credit for a dependent who is a citizen, national, or resident of the United States. To be treated as a resident of the United States, a child generally will need to meet the requirements of a 'substantial presence in the United States' test.

Although most VITA clients do not have this problem, there is in an issue for individuals who have income reported to them as **Non-Employee Compensation**. Such income is reported via 1099-MISC forms for non-employee compensation, with box 7 checked to indicate that the payment was for non-employee compensation. This has been confusing for some clients and seems unfair. This type of payment and payment record is intended by the IRS to be used as a method for companies to hire independent contractors to work specific tasks. For example, if a company is expanding their facilities and needs a painter to paint their new buildings, they may hire an independent contractor to do the work and the company would report payments to that contractor on a 1099-MISC form. Such independent contractors are expected to be fully skilled in their craft, to have the tools necessary to accomplish that craft, and to work without direction on the detailed steps associated with the contracted work. Since such work is typically sporadic, the hiring company is not required to provide the employee with benefits and is not required to withhold Income taxes, Social Security taxes, or Medicare taxes associated with their employment. In essence, a company employing people in this manner is paying a contractor for services to get work done, rather than paying an employee to do the work that needs to be accomplished. While this is a good and needed approach when used appropriately, it causes some VITA clients problems at tax time.

Many VITA taxpayers who are paid in this manner, although being treated as independent contractors, have no employees of their own and the 'contracts' are simply payment for their personal labor. Payments received in this manner requires the taxpayer to file a Schedule C, (Profit or Loss from Business). When individuals receive non-employee compensation, the IRS considers them to be both the employer and the employee. That means they are subject to both the employer and the employee contributions to Social Security and Medicare. For 2014, the self-employment tax rate is 15.3%. The rate consists of two parts: 12.4% for Social Security (old-age, survivors, and disability insurance) and 2.9% for Medicare (hospital insurance). Filing a Schedule C does afford our clients the ability to write off business expenses against their income, which can be a plus if they keep adequate records. While this is fine for individuals who actually do have a small business, it seems unfair for many of our taxpayers who are paid in this manner but really consider themselves to be employees, don't keep track of business expenses, and are surprised when they are required to pay the self-employment tax, having had nothing withheld by their employer for any of those taxes. During my VITA sessions I have had employees from a number of different fields who received such payments. Fields of employment that I've seen include home health care workers, day laborers, construction workers, and painters.

Many taxpayers don't know what they can expense on Schedule C. I've seen a range of taxpayer knowledge from people 1) who don't keep records and expense nothing, 2) to people who keep poor records and guess at expense numbers and thus may include things that are improper, to 3) people who keep good records of business expenses. It is my (unsupported) belief that a number of employers of VITA clients improperly classify workers as independent contractors explicitly to reduce the <u>employers</u> paperwork and tax burdens, without regard to the impact on employees.

For my more recent returns I have printed out a list of Business Codes as well as copies of Schedule C and accompanying discussions about what can be properly expensed. In this class of self-employment taxpayers there are many people who fail to take advantage of business expenses and I believe that there are others who generalize and overstate their expenses. My printed resource materials help a great deal in discussions with such clients.

There are some specific **Tax Rules Associated with Citizenship**. I was surprised at how many non-US-citizens are resident aliens who are required to, and do, file tax returns. In order to file tax returns, such individuals are required to obtain Individual Taxpayer Identification (ITIN) numbers since they are not allowed to get Social Security numbers. Resident aliens are required to follow the same tax rules as U.S citizens. Although they don't have the benefits of citizenship, by filing tax returns they are able to get tax refunds if more taxes have been withheld than they owe. They are also eligible to obtain the Child Tax Credit. Neither they, nor their families, are eligible to obtain EIC benefits or ACA subsidized health care, but they do have automatic exemptions from ACA penalties. Although there are some different rules such as these, VITA volunteers will prepare tax returns for ITIN holders. The United Way of Tarrant County provides assistance for aliens attempting to obtain ITIN numbers at both United Way year-round Free Tax Center sites.

Lawful permanent residents of the United States (green card holders), on the other hand, can get Social Security numbers and are largely treated by the tax code in the same manner as citizens, although they still do not have all of the benefits of citizenship, including participation in the political process. Some individuals have Social Security cards with qualifications. There are different rules for individuals with Social Security cards which state "Valid for work only with

DHS authorization" and those which state "Not Valid for Employment" . If all other EIC requirements are met, the former are eligible for Earned Income Credit while the latter are not eligible for EIC.

Chapter Five: Specific Examples

This chapter provides examples of tax return preparation encounters that I have experienced. Although all of the situations that I describe reflect the circumstances of actual clients and returns that I have processed, all of the names listed are fictitious. In a further effort to ensure client privacy, I have modified dollar amounts and some of the details and have also sometimes merged one of more similar cases into combined cases for these illustrative examples. I've seen so many different variations and people; I have yet to have a day that didn't have some unique and interesting aspect. As may be noted while reading this chapter, the returns described are not organized by subject, issue, or type of taxpayer. The only organization of the materials is a partial organization by the date on which I prepared the returns. The people and cases that I experienced weren't organized; thus this section isn't either.

Not all of the situations that VITA volunteers address are directly associated with taxes. In our VITA site we have had numerous people who stop in to ask for directions, who need to use the restroom, or who are looking for other services which are provided by our host organization, 'Opening Doors for Women in Need'. I'm including the most unusual of those non-tax situations as my first example. I've included it because, while it does not relate to taxes, it does provide a window into the circumstances and life problems of some of our clients.

One evening a couple arrived asking if they could use one of our telephones to check on a sick relative who lives a couple of blocks away. Their relative had not responded when they called previously. When they went to his door to check on him, he did not respond to their knocks on his door or tapping on his windows. Since he was in poor health, they were concerned that he might be lying incapacitated on his floor, unable to answer the phone or unlock his door. After allowing them to make another call, which also received no response, we suggested that they talk to the apartment complex manager. They declined to contact the manager, saying that if the manager finds out their friend is ill, he will be evicted. We then suggested that they contact 911 and have the police come out to perform a welfare check. The couple declined to make that call as well, again because they believed that if their relative still did not respond, the police would contact the manager of the complex to gain entry. After agonizing over the situation and discussing it between themselves in Spanish, the agitated couple finally left, and we never heard any more about the welfare of the elderly gentleman who they were trying to contact. Did he die? Did he leave and tell no one? Why would he be evicted if he was ill? So many questions with no answers. For me this was another reminder of my own relatively happy circumstances. I can't imagine how an eviction for illness could happen to me. Some of our clients have real life problems that are quite beyond my understanding.

In another example a childless married couple for whom I prepared a return left after their return was completed, but asked us to delay filing it. Apparently their income went up from $30K in 2013 to $60K in 2014, and they were expecting a bigger refund. They wanted some additional time to puzzle over the return and determine whether the refund amount we prepared was correct. Although the return appeared correct to us, since they were the taxpayers responsible for the correctness of their return, it was perfectly appropriate for them to delay until they were comfortable that the content was correct. We gave them a paper copy of the return and held the return until they came back a few days later and asked us to complete the filing.

Another couple arrived to have their taxes done. I'll call them Jane and George. As I usually do, I asked if they had used VITA tax services previously, since that typically means they are more familiar with our process and their basic information (names, address, etc.) might already be on file in our computer system. Jane surprised me by answering that she had had her return prepared at our site a week or two before and now they wanted to get George's return done. When I looked at his Intake form, however, George had indicated that he wanted to file 'married'. I asked if the woman with him was his wife and he said yes. Jane then said that she had filed her taxes as a single person. I told them that I couldn't file including Jane on her husband George's return, because in that case she would be filing twice. I told the husband that neither could I file his return, because by VITA rules in Texas (because Texas is a community property state), 'Married Filing Separately' returns are out of scope for VITA. During my preparation process, however, I had asked him for his income documentation and discovered that he had no income. We talked about that for a bit, since on his Intake sheet he had listed an occupation. George said that he had signed up with a temp agency in late 2014 but that they hadn't found work for him yet. Although willing and desiring to work, he had no income in 2014. No income means no taxes. I then explained (and showed the IRS tax table) that he also would get no Earned Income Credit because EIC (as indicated fairly clearly by its title) requires earned income. I suggested that they consider filing an amendment to the return that his wife had filed previously, with the amendment changing from 'Single' to 'Married Filing Jointly' and including him as a dependent. Even if we had found a way to have him file separately, he would have no tax obligation or refund because he had no income. At that point, in this progressively unfolding disclosure of tax information, George informed me that the IRS owed him $600 for a prior year. I asked if he had documentation and told him that we could file tax returns for prior years if he was owed money. I talked to my VITA Site Coordinator who said that we could indeed file tax returns for a prior year but that he would need to ask the IRS for a copy of his filing information from the prior year which showed a $600 refund that had not been paid. They left with the express intent of getting that information from the IRS and returning to our office to file. I never heard from them again and am left wondering how or why someone would   fail to file a tax return when they knew they were owed a $600 refund. I guess I will never know.

I prepared a return for a moderately well-to-do couple with income significantly above the VITA threshold level. Although their income was above the normal range for VITA returns, it was a slow client day and they are long term VITA clients for whom our site had prepared taxes for several previous years. We did their return. One spouse was of retirement age and the other was about the same age and additionally was disabled. They both had Minimum Essential Coverage for health insurance as required by the Affordable Care Act but their son, who is in his late 20s, had no income and no insurance. The husband turned red when he realized that they would need to pay over $500 in penalties for their son's lack of insurance, despite the fact that they had repeatedly told their son that he needed to get insurance. Although they did not verbally say more, it was clear from watching their expressions and non-verbal interactions that they were very frustrated with their son. At least the penalty was less than the maximum $2448 penalty which could have applied if their income had been still higher. Not carrying their son as a dependent was an option but would have cost them his tax exemption for the year.   They are resigned to this year's penalty but are planning for next year. I hope that they come back just so I can see whether their son got insurance or whether they decided to no longer claim him as a dependent. This return provides a perfect example of the tiny windows into other people's lives that VITA tax preparers get to peer through, if only fuzzily. I don't think I would want to be overhearing the dinner table conversation in their home that evening; even second hand stress is hard for me to take calmly.

I prepared a tax return for a 79 year old woman, Inez, who came to our office with her two slightly younger sisters, Maria and Isabel. My client, who struggled with English, had not filed a return in 2013 and was being dunned by the IRS. She owed ~$500 in taxes on a death benefit from her deceased husband. Maria and Isabel were helping their older sibling. I completed Inez' 2014 return and our VITA Site Coordinator told them to go downtown to the Federal office to find out what they need to do for 2013 and to see if they could establish an installment payment plan because Inez could not afford to pay all of the penalty at this time. All three ladies returned the following day. They said that they had spent most of the day at the IRS office. They returned with instructions that they were to prepare tax returns for Inez for several prior years, through 2013. Our Site Coordinator was able to prepare all of those returns for them, helping them greatly. Inez, the taxpayer, did not realize that she should have been filing until this year. Her sisters had not known the situation until recently, and as a result she owed more than $500 for each prior year. The IRS told them how to set up a payment plan to repay the money owed. Although I don't have any sisters, I do have two younger brothers and hope that if I am ever in similar circumstances that my brothers will be as helpful and understanding with me as Maria and Isabel were with their older sister Inez. We need to care for each other and do what we can. This was a heartwarming story of the benefits of family ties.

On a Saturday in late February I arrived a few minutes before 9:00 for the normal 9 – 2 Saturday shift. We already had one client and two more arrived soon after. It looked like it was going to be a busy day. We soon discovered, however, that the fates were against us. TaxWise (our on-line tax preparation software package) was initially up and down sporadically and then was shut down nationwide. When we attempted to log on, we would get a message from the TaxWise support team indicating that they were aware of the problem and were working on it. Their blog indicated that they hoped to be up in an hour. We waited and after about 90 minutes were able to start preparing returns, although the system was still slow and periodically locked up. My client Henry (who was short on sleep and from his own comments had too much to drink the night before) fell asleep in his chair while we were waiting for the tax site to come up. Periodically he would wake up and go out to his vehicle to check on his brother whom he said he had 'kicked out of bed' so he could use their shared car in order to have his taxes done. The tax site finally came up. I finished Henry's tax return, and had it quality checked. I was pleased; at least we would be able to finally print the return and let my client (and his understandably grumpy brother) go on with their lives. However, just before I was able to press the 'print' button, the system went down again and stayed down. The Site Coordinator eventually 'pulled the plug' and decided that we were all going home for the day. With our decision made, after spending fruitless hours in our office, my client decided to leave and have his taxes done on another day at another nearer VITA site, although the new site would need to start the return again from scratch. Resigned to his fate, Henry walked out the door but almost immediately returned after discovering that his brother had gotten angry and gone home with their vehicle. Henry was stranded. While attempting to arrange replacement transportation, the battery on his cell phone died. It took him a few attempts on a borrowed telephone to arrange other transportation.

On the same day the men's room toilet stopped up.

On the same day our Site Coordinator's only client was missing a W2. The coordinator helped the client log onto an IRS web site which can retrieve W2 files that have been sent to the IRS by employers. The clients W2 was not there, and the company where he had worked was not even listed as a company, leaving the client to believe that his employer had pocketed his tax withholdings and had never reported them to the IRS. We assume that his employer had simply paid our client 'under the table'. Since his former place of employment was in another state, and since our TaxWise web site was down, neither he nor we knew what to do. We all went home. To my knowledge he never returned. It was not a good day at the tax office. I could actually say that again. It was not a good day at the tax office.

On another day I prepared a tax return for one couple, Kent and Nancy, who had two teenage children. Kent worked in a critical job for the US Government. While I was entering their taxes we talked about what might happen if there would be a partial government shutdown. We discussed that subject because a main news topic of the day was that Congress was threatening to defund parts of the government if the president didn't back off his position about letting the non-citizen parents of some citizen children stay in the US. Kent's management at his place of employment told him that since his job is critical, he would have to (temporarily) work without pay, which he did not think was fair. Although not immediately and directly associated with taxes, this is an example of the impact that government decisions can have on taxpayers. Some government decisions and programs, like EIC and the child tax credit, are well known and taxpayers can plan their lives around the impacts of those programs. Others, like this potential shutdown, are not predictable but can have major impacts on the lives of people who have limited savings and limited flexibility in their financial lives. Kent opined that the government, if not able to pay, should at least provide impacted employees with credit cards because they have bills to pay. This couple had already been badly impacted during a prior government shut down a couple of years ago. They were badly impacted, even though they eventually got paid, because of cash flow problems. They had bills that they couldn't pay, which impacted their credit rating and they had to pay late fees which were not compensated. This couple provided another example of the uncertainty in the lives of a number of our VITA clients. Although he seemed to have a good job, Kent's statements indicated that he was living on the financial edge. Kent and Nancy's situation was worse than normal because Nancy was permanently disabled. While sitting before me as I entered their tax information, Nancy began to look very unwell; I was concerned we were going to need to dial 911 to address a seizure happening before my very eyes. I now understand why she is on disability. Just another typical atypical day at the tax office.

On another day in February I had only two returns. The first was a return for a young woman who, in late 2014, married a man who is a recent immigrant and still didn't have an ITIN number. Both came in to the office to file a joint return. My Site Coordinator said that getting the ITIN number can be done by the Site Coordinator at the local Catholic Charities VITA site but that it takes quite a bit of documentation. Until the husband received his ITIN number we didn't have an option except to have the woman file as a single person, which I did. The second return was for a young man who had been working out of state in the oil fields as an inspector. He made relatively good money but didn't have health insurance. I gave him ACA information and suggested that he dial 211 soon to get contact information for an ACA Navigator to reduce the penalty that he will otherwise pay next year. His penalty for 2014 was over $100 because 1% of his income was more than the $95 minimum penalty. He also had paid state taxes in the state where he had worked and asked whether his federal taxes could be reduced as a result. (They couldn't because his standard deduction was higher than he could reach if he itemized in order to claim the state tax payment.) After he left, the office was very quiet. I was able to leave early because a second Site Coordinator was also present and three of us weren't needed.

In early March I presided over my first marriage. Did you know that tax preparers can preside over marriages? No? Perhaps you forgot that I live and volunteer in the great state of Texas? In Texas we can preside over marriages, but only under specific circumstances, which require a little explanation. I think this marriage provides an illustrative example of acceptable circumstances. My clients were unmarried when they arrived in our office and were married as they left; I'd say that counts as a marriage in the tax office, wouldn't you? Here is how it happened.

An unmarried couple arrived needing three years of taxes prepared. They arrived with their young and very well behaved son. The young woman, who had good English skills but had never previously filed taxes, asked me if they could file jointly. I asked if they were married, which of course is a prerequisite for them to file as "Married Filing Jointly". She said "No, we are not married, but we've lived together for many years and we'd like to be married". I paused. I then told her that they could file a joint tax return if they wanted to declare that they were married by common law. I explained what that meant and asked her if they wanted to be married in that manner.

A valid common law marriage in Texas occurs when a man and woman become husband and wife without getting a marriage license and having a marriage ceremony. Once established, a common law marriage has the same legal effect as a ceremonial marriage, including the constraint that while they can get married by common law, they cannot subsequently get <u>unmarried</u> without an official divorce and accompanying court action.

Common Law Marriages are legal not just in Texas but also in a handful of other US states, as well as in a number of foreign countries. Texas law is similar to many others, wherein to have a common law marriage you must do three things, besides being of marriageable age and having an opposite sex partner. You must both 1) Agree to be married, 2) Live together as husband and wife, and 3) Publicly present yourselves as being married. One of the valid ways to present yourselves as being married is to sign legal documentation in which you assert that you are married. Thus, by merely asserting to me, as their tax preparer, that they are married and signing a 'Married Filing Jointly' (MFJ) tax return as husband and wife they become married. Say it publicly and it shall be true. Since the joint tax return is filed with the federal government the IRS will henceforth require that the couple file tax returns as married (unless one dies or they get officially and legally divorced).

After explaining how common law marriages work, and the seriousness of that decision, I let the couple think a bit while I entered their tax data. I then asked them again if they wanted to file as husband and wife. They said they did and I completed the return in that manner. I watched as they both signed their 'Married Filing Jointly' return. As they left I congratulated them on their marriage. Given their interpersonal interactions and the presence of their happy and well-adjusted son, I have no doubt that their marriage will be a success and that they will return for many years to have more MFJ returns prepared.

Not all tax clients have such happy circumstances. There are many taxpayers who come in and report living under circumstances that leave me feeling sorry for them, while simultaneously refreshing my belief that I have been, despite my own setbacks, extremely fortunate in my life. The phrase that frequently comes to mind is "There but for the grace of God go I". Things can happen to any of us even though we are good people, try hard, and do nothing bad to merit our misfortunes. One specific example came from a woman who came in to have her taxes done and wanted to know if she could take her adult son as a dependent. Her son had a medical condition which caused her to leave work in order to care for him. She is currently subsisting on Social Security payments and needs to work, but cannot work and also care for son. Without a salary from working, however, she does not have the financial resources to care for him. She is in trouble if she does and in trouble if she doesn't; the classical 'no win' situation. While the tax code certainly does allow adult children to be taken as dependents, she decided not to do so since her son had prior tax debts and, despite medical problems, had made more money on part time jobs than would permit her to claim him. While I could and did provide her with tax code advice and prepared her return, I could do nothing about her underlying situation. The world has many people like her. There but for grace of God go I. We need to be as sympathetic and helpful as we can be.

Later I prepared a return for Debbi, a nineteen year old Texas college student. It was her very first tax return. In addition to being a full time college student, hardworking Debbi had worked for three different employers during the year. I entered information for all three W2s. Because it was her first return and she didn't know what to expect, Debbi had to call her mother to see if her mother was going to claim her as a dependent or whether she should claim herself. Her mother was claiming Debbi as a dependent and accordingly her daughter was not able to file her own 1098-T, but her mother was able to do so. The Form 1098-T, Tuition Statement, reports the amount of qualified education expenses paid by the student during the tax year. It is provided to students by educational institutions and allows taxpayers to determine the educational benefits for which they are eligible on their tax returns.

Debbi's mother came to us on a later day and said that her daughter commented at home that she now understands taxes because the man at VITA (me) had explained it so clearly. Previously she had seen her father prepare the family taxes but he had never involved his daughter in the process and she had no understanding of how the tax system worked. It was a nice reward for me to hear those comments. After the mother related the comments, I lifted my well used, 230 page, VITA Resource Guide, showed it to the mother, and lightheartedly told her that I didn't actually teach her daughter everything about taxes; Debbi might not yet have quite a full understanding of the tax system. This interchange was one of many examples of positive feedback that I got from our clients; feedback that will keep me coming back to provide assistance to others.

During the brightness of one sunny afternoon, with fluffy white clouds providing periodic pockets of shade, while I was studying my Volunteer Resource Guide in preparation for my next client, I heard a number of very sharp noises outside the building. It sounded to me like someone was banging on the glass of our windows. About 30 seconds later I heard another series of the sharp noises. Our Site Coordinator looked out the window and discovered that the noises were in fact gunshots. Two individuals were having a gun battle in the street next to our building! She locked the front door to the building and called the police. Apparently no one was hit, neither bystanders like us nor assailants nor intended victims. After the police arrived we unlocked the doors and continued with business as usual. In retrospect it was just another unexpected adventure during my tax preparation volunteer service.

We had a slow start one day in early March. As I usually did when we had no clients, I began to study aspects of the tax code in which I felt the need of a refresher. I found a training web site for ACA tax preparation. After a quiet period we began to get clients. I remember one set of two unmarried older people who were living in the same house and each filing separate returns. I did his return while our Site Coordinator did her return. Since he had two daughters and claimed that he provided their support I listed his filing status as 'Head of Household'. He had 3 W2s plus unemployment. When we were both done with our data entry, the Site Coordinator and I began to do our normal quality checks of each other's returns. During her review of my return she realized that both clients were living at the same address and both were filing as 'Head of Household' from the same address. My Site Coordinator recognized that since they are living at the same address it is not possible that each of them is paying the majority of household expenses. Only one can be paying the majority and therefore the IRS would likely hold up either one or both returns. After discussions with the taxpayers, we changed his filing status to 'single'. I was about to check whether he would do better if he itemized deductions when my Site Coordinator noticed that his taxable income was already zeroing out, even with just the standard deduction. Since his standard deduction and exemptions were already larger than his income, itemization would not provide a tax refund improvement.

We stopped, checked, and printed his return and both clients left the office as satisfied customers.

One day a female client needed my help. She had two adult dependent sons neither of whom had any income and one of whom was in jail. Although she had health insurance, neither of her sons had the necessary Minimum Essential ACA Coverage. The initial draft of her return showed that she would have to pay the $95 penalty for each son. After my Site Coordinator looked at the return, she realized that the lady could drop the son who was in jail as a dependent. Doing so removed his ACA penalty and did not change anything else on her return because her taxable income was already zeroed out as a result of her deductions and exemptions, even with only one dependent. We completed her return. As she left she said that she planned to contact the marketplace to see if she could get cheaper ACA marketplace coverage because her employer-provided coverage was too expensive. We believe that she is unlikely to be successful in finding more affordable insurance because, although there are a few exceptions, generally a marketplace subsidy is not available to people eligible for other coverage, such as Medicare, Medicaid, or an employer-sponsored plan.

I did a return for a 20-something year old man who came in with his mother. She had previously had her taxes done and was helping him get his done. The client said that he had health insurance for all of 2014 through the ACA marketplace so I entered the 'full coverage' entry, however when I asked him for his 1095-A (Health Insurance Marketplace Statement) he said that he never received one. Without that form I couldn't complete the 8962 (Premium Tax Credit) form to determine if any subsidy that he was receiving was correct, was too high, or was too low. My Site Coordinator called someone and found out through the ACA marketplace that my client had filed for an exemption, but the decision on his exemption and thus any Exemption Certificate Number (ECN) was still pending. Accordingly I entered 'pending' on ACA form 8965 (Health Coverage Exemptions). ACA filing can get really complicated. We filed his taxes but told the client that he needed to talk to the ACA marketplace, partly to fix 2014 but also to ensure that the same problem does not appear in 2015 taxes. In one of the minor oddities of the session, I asked him for a routing number and account number for his bank account, given that he indicated that he wanted to obtain his refund by direct deposit. His mother didn't think he had a direct deposit account, but he said that he did. However, when he couldn't find his account numbers they finally decided that he should have me enter the bank numbers for his mother's account, to which he has access. Oh the strange little things that we see every day!

One of my most memorable clients, from a personal perspective, was an elderly woman who, at over 90 years old, still mows her own lawn. She looked much younger and said that her two sisters both lived to 96. She arrived by herself and was completely aware of her tax situation and finances. Her return itself was simple since her total income was from Social Security and a Teachers Retirement System plan from her deceased husband. I hope to be that fit and that alert when I reach that age . . . if I reach that age. I think the fact that she stays active physically and mentally helps. Besides, she must have a good familial support system and genes if her sisters lived to their mid-90s and she will soon be there herself.

Spanning the range of returns for older individuals, I did a return for a 79 year old, visually impaired man who came in to have his taxes redone. He had his return filed earlier in the tax season and had already received an ~ $700 refund. He obviously filed too early because he later received a statement from his broker with a number of significant financial transactions including a $30K stock sale (at a small loss) and about $8000 in tax exempt interest income. I would guess that he was frustrated with himself when he received that statement, because surely he should have remembered that he sold some stock and would also have interest income. After receiving the brokers combined statement, he went back to his commercial paid tax preparer to have them file a 1040X amendment. According to our client, the preparer seemed to have a lot of trouble with the amended return and it appeared to the client that he had been charged taxes on his tax exempt income (after including that income, his refund disappeared and he instead owed a small amount). Rather than mailing in the 1040X that he received from his tax preparer, he called the IRS and the person to whom he spoke confirmed his opinion that tax exempt investments should not be taxed. The IRS suggested that he come to a VITA site, so he came to us, essentially for a second opinion. I looked at the return, got started entering our own version of the initial return, and then got overwhelmed by the complexity of the broker's statement for the 1040X and asked our Site Coordinator for assistance. She completed the return (while I did another return) and indeed the revised return showed that he would need to return his refund and pay about $70 extra. Afterwards I looked at his return and discovered what had happened. Although he had to pay more taxes, he did NOT have to pay taxes on his tax exempt investment. Instead the income from his tax exempt investment raised his total income past the base amount for his filing status with the result that the amount of his Social Security that was taxed increased up to the 85% maximum. In effect he had to pay more taxes after getting a tax exempt payment simply because of the rules on when Social Security starts charging the max 85% rate on Social Security Benefits. His tax free investment income was not taxed, but its receipt meant that more of his Social Security was taxed. His confusion was understandable because his initial tax preparer obviously had not informed him about why his taxes had increased, and in fact (although it ended with the same number) that prior preparer had entered some amounts into the wrong places, which added to the confusion.

In late March we had a Spanish emphasis day. Except for my first client, everyone else was a predominant Spanish speaker and we had some problems with communication. My last clients of the day, following a very busy first 3 hours, were a man who I will call Carlos and his female friend who wanted to file separate returns, with each of them claiming one child as a dependent. I helped Carlos while our Site Coordinator helped his friend. Because of some conflicts on the intake sheet, I asked Carlos if he was married. He indicated that he wasn't sure (and I'm sure you will agree that being unsure about marriage is a bit unusual). There was no question in his mind that at one time he <u>had</u> been married. There was also no question in his mind that he had attempted to get a divorce. The uncertainty related to the fact that there had been some problems with the divorce and he wasn't sure whether it was finalized or if he was still married. Because of language problems it was a very confusing session. As best as I could determine, the woman who came in with him may or may not have been the woman to whom he may or may not be still married. Regardless, we followed their requests and filed for them as two single people, each with one dependent child. Perhaps this was a case where we should have accessed the available Language Line and involved a bilingual translator, although since Carlos didn't know if he was actually divorced a language line probably would not have helped. Both clients were US citizens and both got EIC payments. My client was a general laborer and had 6 W2s as well as unemployment for the year. As a note, having multiple sources of income is not unusual for our VITA client population. Some of our clients have short term or temporary jobs so it isn't unusual for them to have several W2s, sometimes interleaved with periods of unemployment.

One day I completed a return for a middle aged female client who had many W2s, but otherwise had a simple return. She seemed to be a little scattered in thinking and perhaps had mental focus problems. She came with a friend who answered a number of my questions of the client. As I was entering the tax data, the client and her friend were conversing. In those conversations the client was both talkative and combative in comments about others. She seemed to be a bit out of touch with reality and probably a bit paranoid. She told me that she had problems remembering things. While I was preparing the return she talked about the death of her husband, how she was tired of living in poverty, and how after her husband's death she was taking medications to stabilize her which in turn resulted in her not being able to move on with her life. Her friend was a saint and a blessing for her. Because the client had so many jobs with very short tenure and low pay, I suspect that she may have been terminated from some of those jobs within days of her hire. Although this is purely speculation on my part, her situation seems to provide an example of a person who might have very poor work skills, or might have bad work habits, or might have mental health issues. Any of those problems could make her a candidate to benefit from some of the other social services that United Way or similar agencies offer (through a brief questionnaire) to clients who come in for tax preparation. The chance to communicate availability of other social services is another reason why I have enjoyed volunteering for the VITA program. We directly help people with their specific tax needs and in the process we, through conversation, and through questionnaires, flyers, and brochures, communicate that additional help is available for those willing to access it. Particularly this year with the new ACA program we also serve a very valuable education role to inform clients about how the ACA works and how to benefit from its provisions.

Over a period of a few weeks I processed my first two 'dependent' returns. Both were returns for young people who had, earlier in the year, been claimed by their mothers as dependents because the mothers had provided most of their child's support for the year. In the second case a 17 year old young man came in with his mother, had less than a thousand dollars of income, and wanted help to file his first ever tax return. He was filing in order to get a refund of the taxes that had been withheld from his pay. The return went well and I was able to answer a number of questions providing him (and his mother) with information about how the tax code works. After he had filed I noticed that his standard deduction was a strange number (~$1447) rather than the $6200 standard deduction normal for a single filer. Since his taxable income was zero in any case, an increased standard deduction would not have changed his tax liability. While puzzling about the strange amount for the standard deduction, I remembered that in the prior week I had done my first dependent return for a college student whose standard deduction was also less than $6200. After some discussions with my Site Coordinator and research of the tax code, I subsequently determined the rules for dependent standard deductions. Briefly summarized, they are that dependent filers do not get an exemption (because their exemption was already taken by their parent) but they do get a standard deduction of up to $6200 for a single person. The actual deduction that they get is calculated as their income plus $350, or $6200 (whichever is less) with a minimum standard deduction of $1000. Oh, the wonders of our income tax system! If I, now a trained and IRS certified tax preparer, have trouble making sense of the IRS regulations how could we ever expect the average worker to know how to file? I guess the answer is that we do not expect it; we expect them to get help or use a commercial software package which has many of these rules 'built into' the software.

In late March I had as a client a middle aged disabled woman whose only two items of income were a 1099R disability payment and a Social Security disability payment. Despite her very limited income she had given small contributions to her church and to charity. Her return was simple, but I spent quite a bit of time with her discussing the circumstances under which an itemized return would be appropriate. She had been in section 8 subsidized housing, is getting some other benefits and believes that her life is turning around. This lady was an inspiration to me. Given her circumstances, I was amazed at how cheerful she was and how positive her perspective was about life. I think there are several morals here. Bad things still happen to good people, but staying upbeat and doing the best that you honorably can during trying circumstances can help turn such situations around. People enjoy being around happy and positive people, which in turn can lead to opportunities for the individual in need. It isn't how much you have that leads to happiness, but how you approach and react to your situation that matters the most.

On the last day of March we had a very busy day. I worked three relatively complex returns. Both of the first two returns involved individuals with 1099-MISC returns including only non-employee compensation (box 7 filled in). As such I completed schedule C (Profit or Loss from Business), which provides an opportunity for the client to write off business expenses, but also obligates clients to pay both sides of Social Security and Medical tax. Neither client had kept very good track of their business expenses, perhaps because the clients were essentially employees for larger businesses but were treated by their employers as independent contractors, and thus were obligated to pay their own Social Security and Medical taxes. The first return was for a married couple where the husband was on disability and is now retired. The husband of this couple also had an outstanding IRS debt and my Site Coordinator filled out a form 8379 (Injured Spouse Allocation) which will protect the wife's portion of a tax refund from being taken by the IRS to satisfy the husband's prior tax debt. Although I'd been trained on the usage of the 8379, this return was the first time I had seen it used. That usage is not common but, if you are in that circumstance, it is important that VITA tax preparers are able to offer that refund protection.

The second complex return was for a woman who had existing IRS debt and, since she received non-employee compensation (self-employment) of more than $400 she was required to file a return and pay an approximately $150 penalty because she had no taxes withheld, even though her total income was otherwise much below the filing threshold. She asked why we were filing schedule C (Profit or Loss from Business) since she didn't consider herself to have her own business; she believed that she just worked for another company. Unfortunately for her, the company for which she worked did not give her a salary, but instead paid her as 'non-employee compensation'. After checking with my Site Coordinator, I confirmed that filing schedule C was indeed correct in her case even though it forced her to pay both sides of her Social Security. Although it is possible to enter income obtained via forms 1099-MISC with box 7 checked on 1040 line 21 (Other income), that usage is limited to sporadic employment, etc. and was not appropriate in the client's case. She said that she would call the IRS and add this new debt to the existing IRS debt that she currently owes and already can't pay. She seemed resigned to her tax paying fate, has had similar discussions with the IRS previously, and knew how to handle the situation. As the colorful idiom says, "you can't get blood from a turnip".

On April 1st I had only one client and her case was unfortunately not an April Fool's joke. She was a mid-30 year old resident alien with a Social Security number who was fluently bilingual. She had worked in New Mexico in the prior year but at that time had a low income and hadn't filed for 2013 so she wanted us to do both 2013 and 2014 tax year returns. She married in 2014 and is currently unemployed after moving to Texas. After entering all of the data, we left her 2013 return unfinished because she thought she remembered that she must have had some unemployment income and was going to try to find documentation for that unemployment so it could be added to her 2013 return. She had previously worked for the tax firm H&R Block, but now can't get a job because she is either over or under qualified. She has some college and has worked as an interpreter. She had one W2 and pay stubs for additional payments from a second employer. While in our office she called the second employer and got their EIN number which permitted us to file a 'W2' for that income. Although her income was much below the filing threshold, she is filing because it shows she should get a ~$150 refund for the 2013 tax year. Two days later she returned and said that she had remembered incorrectly and did not have any unemployment income for 2013. Accordingly I completed the 2013 return that I had started two days previously. I then started and completed her 2014 return. Meanwhile the Site Coordinator went above and beyond the call of duty and worked with her on New Mexico State returns. This client's situation is sad because things began to go bad after she got married. She had to move to Texas. She is still without employment. Her husband has been mistreating her, is stalking her, and is very controlling. She no longer wants to be married and doesn't know where to turn. She was caught and distraught. We were able to help her with taxes and our Site Coordinator provided her with information that could help with her deteriorating domestic situation. Sometimes life turns up lemons rather than cherries. Taxes were the least of this client's problems, but at least we were able to remove taxes from her worry list. It was a sad day, but it felt good to be able to help in the areas that I could help.

On April 2, 2015 I had two clients who had received 1098-T Tuition Statements. The first was a school bus driver who was also going to school. She had several W2s plus a 1098-T for which she got a small American Opportunity Credit. The second return was for a single woman with a small 1098-T and no other income. Although she had no income, she did get a small refund because of the Education credit, but she was surprised when she didn't get an EIC payment. I politely explained that she needed to listen to the words 'Earned Income' in EIC. You don't get a credit if you haven't earned any income. This was not an unusual situation. The tax code is complex. I think the 'word on the street' might say that taxpayers may get a large EIC refund, but they don't understand the nuances of lower income requirements and upper income limits that make those refunds vary. Unless you study all the rules, I would guess that the refund or taxes due on returns generally seem somewhat arbitrary to our clients.

On April 7th we had a very busy first 3.5 hours. The Site Coordinator and I each prepared five returns and provided other support as needed. My first client was actually a repeat client. She was a lady who primarily spoke Spanish and whose 'taxes due' return I had done a few weeks earlier. She came back to our VITA site requesting our help to ensure that she would send in her 1040-V (Payment Voucher) payment correctly. She brought everything, a money order made out for the correct amount, her 1040-V form and instructions, a blank envelope, and two stamps (just to be safe). I read the very clear English instructions about what to do and then she, following my detailed instructions, entered 'United States Treasury' as the Payee and wrote her name and Social Security number on the money order, exactly as described by the instructions. I then told her how to address the envelope and watched her put on the stamp. She was/is a sweet lady and her return to our office for this simple purpose gave me a sense of reward and accomplishment. You know that you are providing a valuable service, and doing it with politeness and respect, when people return to have you confirm that they are doing things correctly. She made my day!

Another client had an issue with a missing W2. She came with two W2s but, despite the fact that it was already early April, she was still missing a third W2 from another firm for employment that she had in January. We told the client that she had two choices. One option was that she could have us hold her return until she contacted the IRS for the record of the missing W2, at which point we would file her return. The second option was for her to file without the missing W2. My Site Coordinator indicated that the IRS would likely simply modify the return by including information from that third

W2, and then notify our client about the correction that they had made and the concomitant change to her refund that was entailed. Since it would make no difference in her refund regardless of which option she selected, my client elected to file the return with only information from the two W2s that she possessed. I would have made the same choice (. . before I started volunteering I thought tax preparation would be fairly straight-forward!).

Another return was for a US citizen of recent African extraction (and accent to match). She claimed Head of Household status and had a W2 for less than $3000 of income. She also had thousands of dollars of personal expenses and business expenses, including business expenses for airline travel to the U.S., for a business that she had started but from which she earned less than $200 in income. She asked if we were CPAs and finally decided, with our guidance, that there was no need to itemize her personal expenses even though itemization had been beneficial in the prior several years. Itemization was not beneficial because even her current Standard Deduction and Exemption amounts were zeroing her income. Because this return was complex I asked for assistance from my Site Coordinator. My Coordinator suggested that the client hold most of her business expenses pending and plan to use them as 'carry forward' expenses on her 2015 return in anticipation that her business income would be much greater in the 2015 tax year. If she attempted to use the business expenses now, the losses would subtract from her ordinary income and she would lose her EIC benefit of slightly less than $1000 as a result. No earned income means no EIC. The client kept notes about what to do next year and seemed to leave happy. It seems that no matter how many returns I do, clients come in with unusual situations that I have never considered.

On April 9th I prepared a return for a single client who came in with 2 children. She had lost her decent 2013 medical job when her doctor (boss) retired. She had subsequently started school at Tarrant County College to improve her job skills and employability and between her lost job and hours spent in college had very low income for the 2014 tax year. This client provides an example of how people might need help even though they are responsible and doing everything that they can to overcome their troubles. As a country we want people like her who, when faced with difficulty, take active steps to fight back and do what is necessary to pull themselves up and overcome their fiscal problems. In this client's case, she also had the added burden of being responsible for her children's father. After I completed her return, she told us that she had power of attorney for her male friend who will be in jail until June of 2015. She had all of the necessary paperwork for his tax return and I completed that return as well, with her signing. Although her friend had health insurance for the first part of the year, I used (for my first time) an ACA exemption code of 'F', which is the ACA exemption code for incarcerated individuals, to cover the months of 2014 that he had been in jail.

Oscar came to the site on April 11th, just four days before the filing deadline. He had a simple return, claiming his brother as a dependent. Although trained as a chemist, he had not filed a return for over 10 years because he was staying at home to care for his parents, who have now died. He said that his brother was unemployed last year and now has a manual labor job, but that his brother, although he graduated from high school, cannot read well. As I entered Oscar's three W2s, we found he was eligible for a 138% ACA exemption (to clarify, the 138% exemption is an ACA exemption code 'G' which applies to states such as Texas which have declined to expand their Medicaid program). Oscar was claiming his brother because Oscar provided their total support last year and filing as Head of Household is financially better for him, however he did not have the brother's Social Security card or number. We put the return on hold and Oscar drove back to a nearby small town known as Whiskey Flats to get his brother's Social Security number. When he returned with the card, we realized that one of the numbers on the brother's Social Security card was unreadable. The unreadable number could have been either a 5 or a 3. I looked at it and convinced everyone else that it was a 5. My Site Coordinator proceeded to finish the return, telling Oscar that she would call him if the IRS rejected the return because of an invalid Social Security number. (The IRS subsequently rejected the return because Social Security number was invalid. After changing the number to a 3 it was accepted). This example has conclusively demonstrated that my expertise at divining fuzzy numbers is fallible.

Floyd came in as a repeat client to have his taxes done. He is currently unemployed, but had relatively high income which pushed him over our normal filing threshold. As a result of his two technical jobs, plus unemployment, Floyd owed over $1300 to the IRS. Since he is currently unemployed he will not be able to pay what he owes at this time. He was also not aware of the Affordable Care Act and the penalty that he owes for failure to have health insurance. Although Floyd is currently unemployed, I suggested that he should contact the ACA marketplace for insurance to reduce his ACA Shared Responsibility Payment for 2015. (His penalty for 2014 was running over $40 per month). Floyd had a home and accompanying house taxes and mortgage interest deduction and was able to itemize his deductions.

On the Saturday before April 15th Tax Day, we had a long day. Some people were finally starting to realize that they may owe taxes by the middle of the next week! This long day was supposed to have normal Saturday hours which start at 9:00 A.M. and end at 2:00 P.M. Although we had clients during the day, it was surprisingly not very busy. Shortly before 2:00 P.M. we discovered why. Several people came in just before 2:00 asking for their taxes to be done. When the Site Coordinator told them that we were about to close our Saturday shift, the people who came in said that on Friday the receptionist at the counter had told them that that our hours on Saturday were going to be from 2 until 8! Accordingly a number of people deliberately delayed coming into the office until the afternoon. Upon hearing that unwelcome news the Site Coordinator and I worked (without even a late lunch break) for another two hours to process all of the additional taxpayers who had been misled through no fault of their own. Things happen.

We had several returns of interest during the long day. A man arrived with his borderline senile mother who did not understand why she owed money. A self-employed woman with her own successful small business came in with a very well organized list of expenses and left surprisingly happily even after discovering that she owed thousands of dollars to the IRS. A self-employed grandmother, living on retirement income and caring for her two grandchildren had her taxes completed. A young woman came in to file a dependent return in order to get her tax withholdings returned. During the return preparation we discovered that no one in her family would be able to claim her tuition credit for education expenses because her parents were married but wanted to file separate returns.

On April 14th, the second to the last day of tax season, we had a full lobby when we arrived at 3:00 to start our shift and despite the arrival of two additional tax preparers and two intake volunteers, we extended our closing hours beyond 8:00 P.M. (until about 9:30) to handle later arrivals. My most memorable client of the eight that I handled was a couple filing jointly who arrived with two small children, including a 2 year old who was loud, disruptive, and acted just like a two year old.

As I relate this incident, remember that, as a volunteer, things like this might happen to you. These clients arrived after I had about 4 hours of nonstop client service, with no opportunity to eat my granola bars, and I don't do very well when my blood sugar level is low. Their return was relatively straightforward although the husband had received (for the first time) non-employee compensation and didn't realize that he could write off expenses. I provided them with some information and while I was entering the remainder of the information they were summarizing his schedule C expenses. Meanwhile the small child was all over the room, the room was full of clients and the return was taking longer than expected to prepare. When I finally got it done, I printed a review copy and discovered that the printed version did not agree with the screen version! I have no certain explanation for how this happened, but I tried to print again and got the same result. I'm convinced that it was a software problem, triggered by a very unique set of circumstances. I think this happens because the screen version has more questions and more information than appear in the printed version. Thus the printout is not just a copy of the screen, but rather is a separately generated copy from the same source data. Of all times to have this happen, this was the worst; long day, everyone tired, kids uncontrolled, low blood sugar, it was bad. The husband had already left for work and the wife and kids were about to go home but the printed tax return showed a refund ~$500 less than the screen version that I had discussed with the clients. In desperation, I finally closed the return and reopened it. After doing that the problem went away, but all of my Schedule C independent contractor information had disappeared. I reentered it. After reentering that information the refund went down another $500.00. I would have been 'tearing my hair out', except that I am already bald. After a bit more sleuthing I discovered that there were now two schedule Cs on the return. I deleted the duplicate schedule C and the refund, in both the printed and electronic versions, returned to the original higher value and I was able to print the correct return and have it signed. As I was getting the final correction made, the wife was on the telephone to her husband telling him he needed to come back to the office, a request that I, just in the nick of time, was able to head off. Although the worst part of the problem was not due to the clients, I was relieved to see them go, with

61

the episode ended. Remember again, as a volunteer tax preparer, things like this could happen to you!

And Finally . . Tax Day Arrived! The day was too busy to keep good notes about clients, but one of my clients on that day, who I will call Gloria, was a single woman who had a return which encapsulated several issues faced by a number of VITA clients during this tax season. As a way to wrap up this chapter on examples, I think some comments about her return will be useful.

Gloria was college educated and had a good-paying job for the first few months of 2014.   Subsequently she lost her employment and through various causes is now trying to survive by running her own business doing event planning and preparation for other organizations. She had been on affordable housing and qualified for heavily discounted telephone service through the Federal Communications Commission's 'LifeLine' service discussed in Chapter 6. That LifeLine telephone service is essential for her to run her small business. She is educated, smart, well organized and has a lot of initiative.   Nevertheless, in her words, she would likely have become homeless if someone had not gifted her with a travel trailer. In this first year of her small business she had only limited income and few business expenses. She had applied to the ACA marketplace and was pleased when she was informed that she qualified for highly subsidize health insurance.

As I entered Gloria's income and expenses, things began to unravel and look less rosy. We realized that she didn't have enough receipts to itemize deductions.   What was much worse was that as we calculated her ACA Premium Credit we realized that although Gloria had ACA coverage, her subsidy had been far too high. When her salaried income from the first few months of 2014 was added, she had received much more income than the marketplace had projected and accordingly was required to repay more than $1000 of the ACA subsidy that she received. Her financial situation was far too fragile to repay that kind of tax bill all at once. Per my suggestion, she said that she would make a good faith payment on her tax bill to show her positive intent to pay her debts and then she would contact the IRS to set up a payment plan. Hopefully her subsidized cell phone service will allow her to keep up her business, which in its second year should begin to bring in more income.

This chapter of specific examples completes Part ONE of the book. I have found that there have been interesting and unusual situations and tax challenges every day of my volunteer service. These variations are what keep my volunteer service interesting and fulfilling. I have also found that my growing level of experience is making me more comfortable in preparing returns and has allowed me to sometimes assist other tax preparers in situations where I happen to know how something works that they have either not known or have forgotten. I've made a difference in our clients lives. I'm glad I did it. I plan to volunteer again next year.

The next part of this book provides additional historical information and commentary about how we could make the tax preparation process and the tax codes better.

PART TWO: Tax Options

Chapter Six: Tax Code and Social Program History

I have found that some aspects of our current tax code are, in my subjective opinion, unnecessarily troublesome. I believe that the overall tax code is good and well intentioned, but time and circumstances sometimes conspire to thwart good intentions. As T.S. Eliot reportedly said, "Most of the evil in this world is done by people with good intentions."

In this second part of the book, Part Two, I transition from 'just reporting the facts as I know them' to more subjective observations. In these chapters I document the insights that my tax preparation experience has provided me and summarize some thoughts for potential tax code improvement.

Readers who are only interested in the facts about the VITA program, and what it is like to participate as a volunteer, do not need to read Part Two. It provides additional factual background about some of the key tax codes; it interleaves comments about why the tax code exists as it is; and it discusses some alternative ways in which the objectives of our society could be met. I begin with comments about the origins of some VITA relevant tax codes and their objectives. Unless we know or can divine the intent of current tax provisions, we have no basis to critique those provisions or provide suggestions.

Because I am writing from the perspective of the tax system as it affects lower and middle income people, you will see that most of the relevant tax codes are codes which address the government's decisions over the years to provide an appropriate level of tax burden for different segments of society. Most of the provisions important to VITA clients are provisions which implement progressive taxation; that is, those taxpayers who have more resources and income are expected to pay more in taxes, with progressively higher tax burdens and tax rates as income climbs.

There are numerous ways that our progressive tax code is currently implemented. We have already discussed many of them. A basic means of implementing progressive taxation is through the explicit assessment of higher tax rates for higher income people. Another way is to totally exclude the first portions of income from taxation via the Standard or Itemized Deduction, and tax code Exemptions. These deductions and exemptions exclude thousands of dollars of income from taxation for all taxpayers, regardless of income. The more members that there are in a tax family, the higher the amount of exclusion. Although these mechanisms are available at all income levels, they are most beneficial (from a percentage of income perspective) at lower levels of income. In addition to these basic leveling mechanisms, our federal tax code provides explicit mechanisms intended to help the disadvantaged, including the EIC, CTC, and ACA that were discussed in prior chapters as well as other societal welfare programs including Food Stamps (now known as SNAP (Supplemental Nutrition Assistance Program)) and the WIC (Women, Infants, and Children) program.

We then move to tax provisions which may not be progressive but instead are intentionally implemented to foster certain societal goals. Examples of these affect all income levels, but are more generally beneficial to specific groups (and as such are frequently subject to lobbyist attention). Examples are beneficial tax treatment for higher education, benefits for married people filing jointly (and penalties for married people filing separately), tax benefits for home ownership, tax benefits for small businesses, benefits for mineral depletion, tax benefits for religious organizations, tax credits for energy efficiency, and tax beneficial programs such as Individual Retirement Accounts (IRAs) to encourage retirement savings. Some of these provisions are beneficial to the typical VITA client, while many are not. For example, IRAs or 401Ks are usable at all income levels but they are of no value to people who are 'living hand to mouth' and whose income is needed to support their lives, with no ability to save. Similarly tax benefits for home ownership are of no benefit to citizens who do not have enough financial resources or stability to own a home.

Despite explicit attempts to be progressive, we are seeing increasing levels of income inequality in the country. Restated, rather than our taxation and economic systems leveling the playing field, the rich are still getting still richer and the poor are getting poorer. The following paragraphs summarize some of the important tax codes that affect VITA clients. Included information was obtained from the IRS, the Congressional Research Service (which provides policy and legal analysis to committees and Members of both the House and Senate) and other web sites. The findings provided in these paragraphs are just summaries and do not cover some of the intricacies and exceptions of these tax laws. Readers should accordingly do their own research, in view of their own circumstances, if planning any actions related to the provided information.

Because **welfare benefits** are generally not required to be listed as income and thus are not taxable, there are virtually no impacts on the tax codes as a result of welfare programs. Nevertheless, I am including a section on welfare because the need for, and usage of, welfare benefits is a common situation for VITA clients. We can't really understand other tax code provisions related to social services without understanding the welfare system.

The moral and ethical requirement to help the disadvantaged goes back to the beginnings of humankind. Much more recently, but still long ago, recognition of the need for welfare has existed since the start of the United States. The following edited excerpts of the history of welfare in this country were taken from http://www.welfareinfo.org/history/.

Welfare in the United States commonly refers to the federal government welfare programs that have been put in place to assist the unemployed or underemployed. Help is extended to the poor through a variety of government welfare programs that include Medicaid, the Women, Infants, and Children (WIC) Program, and Aid to Families with Dependent Children (AFDC).

The history of welfare in the U.S. started long before the government welfare programs we know were created. In the early days of the United States, the colonies imported the British Poor Laws. These laws made a distinction between those who were unable to work due to their age or physical health and those who were able-bodied but unemployed. The former group was assisted with cash or alternative forms of help from the government. The latter group was given public service employment in workhouses.

Throughout the 1800's welfare history continued when there were attempts to reform how the government dealt with the poor. Some changes tried to help the poor move to work rather than continuing to need assistance. Social casework, implemented by caseworkers visiting the poor and training them in morals and a work ethic, was advocated by reformers in the 1880s and 1890s.

Prior to the Great Depression, the United States Congress supported various programs to assist the poor. One of these, a Civil War Pension Program, was passed in 1862 and provided aid to Civil War Veterans and their families.

Under President Franklin D. Roosevelt, the Social Security Act was enacted in 1935. The Act established a number of programs designed to provide aid to various segments of the population. Unemployment compensation and AFDC are two of the programs that still exist today.

68

A number of government agencies have been created to oversee welfare programs. Some of the agencies that deal with welfare in the United States are the Department of Health and Human Services (HHS), the Department of Housing and Urban Development (HUD), the Department of Labor, the Department of Agriculture, and the Department of Education.

The US welfare system stayed in the hands of the federal government for the next sixty-one years. Many Americans were unhappy with the welfare system, claiming that individuals were abusing the welfare program by not applying for jobs, by having more children just to get more aid, and by staying unmarried so as to qualify for greater benefits. Welfare system reform accordingly became a hot topic in the 1990's. In 1996 President Bill Clinton signed the Personal Responsibility and Work Opportunity Reconciliation Act which had been passed by a Republican Congress. Under the act, the federal government gives annual lump sums to the states to use to assist the poor. In turn the states must adhere to certain criteria to ensure that those receiving aid are being encouraged to move from welfare to work. Though some have criticized the program, many acknowledge it has been successful.

In addition to the above assistance, and not normally considered as part of welfare, since 1985 the Federal Communication Commission has also sponsored and supported the 'Lifeline' program for discounted telephone service for qualifying low-income consumers to ensure that all Americans have the opportunities and security that phone service brings, including being able to connect to jobs, family and emergency services. In 2005, Lifeline discounts were made available for pre-paid wireless service plans in addition to traditional landline service. To qualify, consumers must either have an income that is at or below 135% of the federal Poverty Guidelines or participate in an assistance program such as Medicaid, Food Stamps, Section 8 Housing, or Temporary Assistance for Needy Families (TANF).

The Federal government's TANF program is currently implemented through grants given to each state to run their own welfare programs. Although there are state level variations on these rules, to help overcome the former problem of unemployment due to reliance on the welfare system the federal TANF grant requires that all recipients of welfare aid must find work within two years of receiving aid. This requirement includes single parents who are required to work at least 30 hours per week and married parents who jointly must work 55 hours per week. There is also a 5 year lifetime limit on aid. Failure to comply with work requirements can result in loss of benefits.

The type and amount of aid available to individuals and dependent children varies from state to state. When the Federal Government gave control back to the states there was no longer one source and one set of requirements. Most states offer basic aid such as health care, food stamps (now known as the Supplemental Nutrition Assistance Program (SNAP)) , child care assistance, unemployment, cash aid, and housing assistance.

As described in Chapter 4, the **Earned Income Credit (EIC) and the Child Tax Credit (CTC)** are two tax provisions targeting low- and moderate-income taxpayers. The EIC encourages work among low-income individuals. Both the EIC and the CTC significantly reduce taxes on low- and middle-income families with children.

The EIC (previously known as the EITC) was enacted during the Ford administration by the Tax Reduction Act of 1975. Originally, the Earned Income Tax Credit (EITC) was supposed to be a temporary refundable tax credit for lower-income workers to offset the Social Security payroll tax and rising food and energy prices. The credit was made permanent by the Revenue Act of 1978. The EITC was considered both an anti-poverty program and an alternative to welfare because it incentivized work. It was later substantially expanded by President Reagan.

The child tax credit was created in 1997 by the Taxpayer Relief Act to help ease the financial burden that families incur when they rear children. Changes in 2001 and 2009 doubled the value of the credit per child up to $1000 and made the credit partially to fully refundable [as an Additional Child Tax Credit] for families earning over $3000. Portions of the law addressing the additional child tax credit will, unless further modified, expire at the end of the 2017 tax year.

Although the Child Tax Credit applies to families of all income levels which have earnings above the income floor for the credit, the same approach does not apply for the earned income credit. The EIC is explicitly targeted to assist low and moderate income earners. There is no EIC benefit if the taxpayer has no earned income. There is also no EIC benefit for taxpayers who (in general) make more than about $45,000. The EIC benefit rises with the number of children in the tax household until it plateaus in the $20,000 income range and then begins decreasing to zero. The exact numbers at which the peak payment is reached and when the payments reduce to zero depend on taxpayer filing status and number of children. Even taxpayers with no children (and low incomes) can be eligible for the EIC, although at much lower payment levels than for taxpayers with children. *Note: Much of the information in this section on the EITC has been excerpted and reworded from the Economic Policy Institute report listed in the Bibliography.*

Since this chapter is talking about ways in which poorer individuals can get societal support, I am including a few comments about other, non-governmental, ways such support can be provided. A **Non-Governmental Organization (NGO)** is an organization that is neither a part of a government nor a conventional for-profit business. NGOs may be funded by governments, foundations, businesses, or private persons. Many provide social support. From the beginning of time people in trying circumstances have received help from individuals and private organizations. Such help ranges from family member helping other family members, to friend helping friend and neighbor helping neighbor. It grows to churches and fraternal organizations establishing help programs for the less fortunate in their communities as well as across the world. As the scale of the need expands, such private non-governmental programs get progressively more difficult to fund, manage, and coordinate. Public/private partnerships begin to step in at this level, engaging private citizens in efficient development and delivery of support services. Although some public/private partnerships are partially funded by the government, many have no government involvement or funding. Even without direct public funding, the US tax code recognizes the importance of NGO organizations by providing exemptions from taxation for those organizations that meet requirements, as through section 501(c)(3) of the Internal Revenue Code.

Finally, there is a level of services for the public good that is so large in scope and so pervasive that our citizens generally agree that they should be directly funded and run by the government. Although some would still argue about the degree of government control and funding (whether national, state-wide, or local) that is needed and advisable, in general our society agrees that the national government should fund, manage and run standing military services for our protection. We also generally agree that we should have the government (at the local level) provide free public schooling for our children. We agree that there should be a government provided infrastructure of roads, waterways, airports, utilities, courts, jails, etc.

Although there has always been discussion about the kinds and levels of services that should be provided directly by the government, there is a general understanding that such services are desirable and necessary in our complex society, and in fact are frequently the most efficient and effective way to provide certain services to our population. One of the recent government initiatives of this type addresses health care and is discussed in the next paragraphs.

The **Patient Protection and Affordable Care Act** was signed into law by President Obama in March of 2010 and as such has only a short history. Its major provisions went into effect on Jan. 1, 2014, although significant portions went into effect before that date and change is expected to continue in years to come.

The Act affirms "the core principle that everybody should have some basic security when it comes to their health care," as President Obama said at the signing. The act is commonly known as the **Affordable Care Act (ACA)** — and widely nicknamed Obamacare. The Act extends insurance to more than 30 million uninsured people, primarily by expanding Medicaid and by providing federal subsidies to help lower- and middle-income Americans obtain health care coverage from private firms. Because the VITA tax client population is generally in this demographic, and because many of the ACA penalties and exemptions are implemented via tax law, the ACA is a major element of most VITA prepared tax returns. The next two chapters provide significant additional comments about the ACA and other tax related programs.

Chapter Seven: Thoughts About Tax Codes

Every person has the responsibility to understand the tax provisions that apply to them and has the opportunity to arrange their business dealings and lives in ways that minimize their tax burden. There is nothing legally or morally wrong if people manage their affairs to minimize their tax burden. As anyone can tell from paying attention to the news, wealthy individuals and businesses regularly hire tax lawyers and lobbyists to minimize their tax exposure, sometimes by arranging their affairs to lower or delay their taxes and other times by attempting to influence legislation which will provide them with tax benefits.

The opportunity to seek tax efficiency sometimes results from unintended aspects and inconsistencies in the tax laws and sometimes because the US Government explicitly uses tax provisions to encourage or restrict certain behaviors. The creation of tax credits for purchasers of electric cars and for energy efficiency additions to homes are examples of explicit government actions to foster desired behaviors. The imposition of federal taxes on cigarettes is an example of the government's usage of the tax code to reduce harmful personal behaviors. While one can argue whether the government should be using the taxation system for such attempts to change behavior, the fact is that the tax system has myriad provisions of this kind. It is also true that wealthy people and businesses pay explicit attention to these rules and change their behaviors so as to reduce their tax burden. While the complexity of the tax code provides many opportunities for dishonest people to defraud the government, there are many perfectly legal and legitimate ways to reduce taxes by thoughtful compliance with current tax laws. As an example at the individual taxpayer level, each tax filer may choose to take either the Standard Deduction or they may itemize their deductions. To the extent that taxpayers can shift the tax years in which they pay expenses that can be itemized, e.g. property taxes or charitable contributions, they may be able to reduce their total tax burden by taking the standard deduction in one year and scheduling payment of expenses that can be itemized into another year.

The typical VITA client also faces many tax provisions that affect their lives, provisions with sometimes obscure and difficult to assess constraints. The difference between VITA clients and big business or wealthy taxpayers is that the typical VITA client has neither the knowledge nor the financial flexibility necessary to maximize their tax refunds or reduce their tax liability. The following paragraphs provide some thoughts about tax codes which affect VITA clients and some options to potentially improve benefits or avoid negative impacts. I'll start with a discussion of the ACA.

The implementation of the **Affordable Care Act (ACA)** is excessively complex, including tax office impacts. Politics and the political necessity to have a major role for private enterprise have made it cumbersome. There are nineteen different types of exemptions of which twelve can be claimed during tax preparation time. As VITA tax preparers, we have been thrown into the middle of a health care political war, forced to explain to taxpayers why they owe penalties if they do not have health coverage and forced to calculate appropriate health care subsidy premiums or identify valid taxpayer exemptions. It seems inappropriate to require tax preparation organizations to address all of this complexity.

As I have discussed in other chapters, most VITA taxpayers do not like the ACA, still believe insurance is unaffordable, and would rather not be forced to do something for which many don't have the funds to realistically pay. Additionally, in Texas as in many other states, Medicaid qualification levels were not expanded to higher income levels, therefore large segments of the low income population can and do get exemptions, which means that the health burden for those individuals stays with the public health system funded by our taxes, thus missing some of the intended benefits of the ACA legislation.

75

Some additional problems with the ACA as currently implemented are:

- The ACA is complex and costly to administer and manage due to the myriad providers, the overhead of exchanges, the processing of subsidies, and the variability of state-by-state implementation.
- Although the ACA provides five levels of choices for coverage (Bronze, Silver, Gold, Platinum, and Catastrophic), no level is a good choices for individuals of limited means. Plans with lower premiums have higher copays, while plans with low copays have high premiums.
- Since many VITA clients have uncertain or unstable employment, accurate income forecasts (and thus premium subsidy forecasts) for those individuals are not possible.
- Correct subsidy values and final determination of exemptions cannot be quantified until tax season of the following year. This results in financial uncertainty for taxpayers and complexity for tax preparers.

Although the ACA has problems, as a society we need to do something to improve our health care system because:

- Medical problems are one major cause that taxpayers lose their jobs and become financially insolvent, possibly becoming a drain on society.
- Adults who do not have insurance are more likely to forego preventive care, thus leading to later incidents of serious health problems which require expensive intervention. As the saying goes, "An ounce of prevention is worth a pound of cure."
- Individuals who obtain care in hospital emergency rooms likely have longer wait times to get care. Further, because emergency rooms must be able to handle serious incidents, delivery of routine care in that environment may come at a higher cost to

society than if they had regular medical care in a more appropriate environment.

- Although the children of VITA clients generally have health care, frequently through Medicaid or the Children's Health Insurance Program (CHIP), the necessity for many individuals to have their children provided healthcare through Medicaid and CHIP adds cost and complexity.

As a philosophical statement, I believe that medical treatment for basic health should not be considered as a luxury item. That is (remember that cosmetic and other discretionary and elective procedures are outside of ACA provided basic care) people don't <u>plan</u> to get sick or need surgery. Accordingly, with few exceptions, health care benefits are not considered by the recipient or the funding taxpayers as frivolous and luxury items. Basic health care is not a want, but rather is a need. People don't <u>want</u> health care (if they are well) in the same way that they might want a big screen color television. People who are sick or need medical care to allow them to go to school or keep their job <u>need</u> that health care to keep their families together and to prevent them from falling into situations where they require the support of other social programs. They need health care to keep their lives together. As a society we need them to be healthy to prevent them from becoming a drag on society. Every individual who we can keep productive is an individual that the society as a whole does not need to help support.

The **Head of Household tax filing status** is one of a number of different filing status choices. Filing as Head of Household provides an additional amount of Standard Deduction dollars in comparison to filing as a single person. For individuals who are not married, but have dependents that they support, filing as Head of Household can be advantageous from a tax perspective, because it can lower a household's amount of taxable income

I find that some of the rules addressing qualification for Head of Household status seem unfair to lower income people. (Of course, even if the rules seem unfair to me, they are the law and I and other VITA volunteers are required to follow the law as written, not as we personally think it should have been written.) The rules seem unfair in situations where two (or more) individuals with dependents are living together in one dwelling and share household expenses. If they each had their own dwelling, they would each be able to file as Head of Household. If they are having trouble making ends meet and decide to live in the same home, sharing expenses, then only one can file as Head of Household. This seems unfair. As another example, let us imagine a case where three sisters, each with children, are sharing a home. If they share expenses nearly evenly, then <u>none</u> of the three sisters will be able to file as Head of Household because none of them will have paid more than half of the costs of the home. Remember also in the calculation of shared costs that TANF funds, housing subsidies, and support from other public assistance programs cannot be counted as part of the taxpayer share of paid expenses. I don't think that our tax rules should be penalizing people for living together if they can have a better standard of living when they live together. I think there are both personal and societal benefits of shared support from others.

Chapter 6 presented some history and facts about **the EIC and CTC**. A review of the program's problems and successes presented in this section have been excerpted and reworded from an Economic Policy Institute report on the topic.

I want to expand a point made in Chapter 6 that the EIC, as opposed to welfare, incentivizes work. Welfare by itself is not only expensive but it is generally viewed unfavorably by those (other taxpayers) who must fund it. The more serious problem, however, is that it can lead to a generational cycle of sustained poverty. The few individuals with low ethics will be happy to take advantage of welfare benefits forever. Those recipients thought processes could be, 'Why should I work to support my family if I can do nothing and get supported by others?'. Individuals with a higher ethical standard, who nevertheless need welfare support through no fault of their own, can have their self-esteem and feelings of self-worth debased by the need to accept handouts from others or the government. The EIC, TANF, and other similar programs endeavored to change those circumstances by more clearly providing short term support to those who are working or doing their best to improve their situations so that they can become self-supporting. As a society we don't want a system divided between the givers and the takers. We want all segments of society to have a stake in the system and to be making contributions to the common good. As the saying goes, it is better to give than to receive; that dictum applies at societal as well as individual levels.

In addition to the changes to CTC coming in 2018 as discussed in the prior chapter, more changes to these social programs should be expected. Changes are expected because at the US congressional level there is a lot of attention being paid to the US debt and deficit and about the unsustainability of many of our social programs, including the Social Security program as well as the programs which we have been discussing. Discussions about broad-based tax reform have focused much attention on eliminating or scaling back tax expenditures— including changes to special tax rates, deductions, exclusions, exemptions, and credits, including the EIC and CTC, that reduce tax liability. Given this, and given past criticisms of these tax credits targeted to low- and moderate-income taxpayers, it would be surprising if the EIC and CTC are not discussed further in Congress to ensure that the money being allocated to these programs is money well spent.

The primary purpose of taxes is to fund government so it can meet various social and economic goals regarding national security, economic stability, income distribution, poverty alleviation, and the efficient allocation of resources. The activities directed to lower-income individuals and families typically involve grants or transfer payments, which are often means-tested. Means-tested grants are fairly effective in reducing poverty but can potentially create work disincentive effects.

This book, in several chapters, has discussed **tax code benefits for lower to middle income people**. While the benefits are certainly beneficial to that group, we should not draw the conclusion that our overall tax system is biased in favor of that group of taxpayers. Some counter examples which favor higher income rate people are itemized deductions, Individual Retirement Accounts, Capital Gains tax rates, Home Energy tax credits, sales taxes on new cars in Texas, rebates for electric cars, and mineral depletion allowances. In my experience these provisions rarely benefit VITA clients.

Chapter Eight: Possible Solutions

In prior chapters I've described how the VITA program works. I've also discussed circumstances that VITA taxpayers face and talked about the complexities of preparing their tax returns. This chapter provides candidate solutions for three areas where tax code changes could simplify and help the VITA client base. The three areas that I target are 1) Non-Employee Compensation, 2) Head of Household Filing Status, and 3) Health Care Coverage and the ACA. I'm sure that there can be many arguments about whether the issues behind these topics are valid, and if valid, whether the solutions that I propose are appropriate corrective responses. This chapter provides my recommendations to make things better.

I want to start the chapter by further discussing some tenets of my philosophy. Rather than espousing partisan positions, I believe that we should be looking at the long term costs and benefits to the client population and to society as a whole, relative to solutions for every issue. When deciding what to do, we should always do a 'long term thought test'. Sometimes our good intentions result in bad and unpredicted side effects. For example, at one point in our history, in a laudable effort to reduce welfare costs and break the cycle of welfare dependency, this country imposed 'man-in-the-house' rules. Agencies in many states following that rule withheld welfare if a working age male was present in the household. As a result, in many two parent households the male left the family so that the mother and children could get benefits. In 1968 the U.S. Supreme Court struck down the regulations as being contrary to the goals of the Aid to Families of Dependent Children (AFDC) program. Although they may have reduced short term welfare costs, as a negative side effect 'man-in-the-house rules' also increased the prevalence of dysfunctional single parent families, thus directly tearing the social fabric of our culture. The damage of those rules was much worse than any benefit gained.

My personal philosophy is driven by a search for long term effectiveness and efficiency in tax utilization and government services. I don't mind paying taxes as long as the taxes are applied to reach desirable long term goals, are effective and efficient in reaching those goals, and as long as the policies being implemented don't have untenable negative side effects.

In the previous two chapters I've discussed the history and rationale for some of the taxes codes that impact VITA clients. I've talked about some issues and complexities that currently exist. The purpose of this chapter is to present a 'thought piece' that could address some of the current difficulties while attempting to adhere to the objectives of the current tax code.

I believe that most people feel that there should be fairness in the amount of taxes that are assessed and collected, even if there is a lot of dissension about what 'fairness' means. There is also little debate about whether we would like our tax process to be efficient. That is, we generally believe that the tax laws should be simple and that the process to assess and collect taxes should be easy, quick, low cost, and not subject to interpretation and vagaries of perspective of individual tax payers or tax preparers. We want taxes done right, done well, and with the lowest possible cost. For the remainder of this chapter I am accepting as a given that in the future we will want to continue to have a progressive system of taxation and that we will want to provide assistance, partially through the tax code, to the less financially able individuals in our society. I believe that we will want to continue to support programs which provide our children with supportive environments and a good educational system. I believe that we will continue to want to provide help to taxpayers of limited means who are trying their best to contribute to society. We will want to continue to help those who are employed as best as their circumstances permit so as to allow them to pay their own way and not have to rely upon help from other people, groups, or governments. Accordingly I am not recommending dramatic changes to the our social philosophy of being willing to help others. The poor will always be with us and we should help as we can. If changes to tax policy can help, they should be considered.

I propose, however, to make some significant changes in how current tax services are provided. Given my prior personal experience as well as my experience as a VITA volunteer, I believe that our current taxation system is the opposite of transparent. It is not simple to understand and it is high in cost and complexity. I think, with some political will and willingness to tackle head-on some 'sacred cows' of our USA philosophy, that we can significantly simplify our social programs and make them much more cost efficient. I further believe that a number of current issues with the tax code are interrelated. One thing affects another.

Let's start with a basic premise of social support programs. We are willing to help people who try to help themselves. We want our support programs to help people who are truly in need, especially those who are in need through no fault of their own. In the process, however, we do not want our support programs to increase dependence of individuals nor to establish an expectation of indefinite future support for citizens or their families. We do not want to foster a cycle of continued dependence which is endemic and lasts from generation to generation, causing the individuals who are being helped to lose their self-motivation. Nor do we want to cause individuals who help by paying the taxes or volunteering to help to become resentful and bitter. We also want a system which provides support in areas that we consider essential, rather than providing benefits that are luxuries or frivolous. Further, we want to provide benefits that are beneficial in the long term, not just for a few months or years. Although there is, and always will be and should be, debate about which benefits fit these criteria, some benefits such as providing supportive environments and adequate housing, food and education for children are examples of the type of benefits that we can support. We want to break the generational cycle of poverty and the generational cycle of criminality. Since an ounce of prevention is worth a pound of cure, we should focus on benefit programs which will make future citizens civic-minded and well-adjusted, as well as making them more prolific earners and taxpayers, because so doing will allow us to spend less on social programs in the future. Having fewer people with low incomes, who are getting fewer benefits, and who are paying more taxes, will be better for all of us and better for society.

So, assuming that we can agree on the goals that I have stated, the question then becomes how we do it and whether there are any relationships between that how and the taxation system that I've been discussing. I think the answer to that question is that there is a relationship. I want to focus on areas where the tax program can be changed to better meet those goals.

We should consider changes to three areas of the tax code. Those areas are 1) Non-Employee Compensation, 2) the Head of Household filing status option, and 3) The Affordable Care Act. I've discussed the problems for our VITA clients in each of those areas in earlier chapters. I cover candidate changes for the Non-Employee Compensation and Head of Household suggestions first, because the ACA recommendations are much more complex to explain.

Non-Employee Compensation: As described in previous chapters, a number of our VITA clients receive income as 'Non-Employee Compensation', reported for taxes on form 1099-MISC, although they don't really have their own independent contractor business. This is confusing and expensive for them. The problem could be fixed in several ways. The rules (or enforcement of current rules) could be changed so that taxpayers with this problem are treated as employees, rather than as independent contractors. Alternatively or additionally, such individuals could be given more information by their employers about the implications of their independent contractor status. Specifically they should be told that they should keep track of their employment related expenses (transportation, mileage, telephone, uniforms, etc.) so that they can accurately deduct those expenses when they file their taxes. They should also be told that they will need to pay self-employment taxes when they file their return and that their employer is not responsible for job related injuries or disabilities if they get hurt while at work. Thirdly, the IRS could clarify tax preparation instructions and allow individuals in this category who do not have claimable expenses to list income of this type as 'other income' and enter it on form 1040 line 21. Before the third suggestion would be implemented, careful consideration would need to be given to the impact of that approach on Social Security eligibility of taxpayers since the 'other income' category would not result in the payment of appropriate amounts into the Social Security and Medicare trust funds.

Head of Household Filing Status: I believe that the Head of Household filing status, while largely achieving its goal of providing some tax relief for taxpayers who are the main providers of a home, food, and basic support services for their tax families, should be eliminated. As described in Chapter 4, the proper determination of whether individuals meet the criteria for this status can be difficult to determine and is subject to abuse or fraud because its correctness is difficult to verify. Further, as I pointed out in Chapter 7, I believe that the restrictions on this filing status unnecessarily and inappropriately discriminate against individuals with children who choose to improve their lives by sharing a home. Our tax policies should foster social values of which our society approves, not penalize and complicate the lives of other individuals who are caught in the unintended consequences of the regulations.

While I am suggesting that the Head of Household filing status should be eliminated, we should also make concurrent changes to Exemption values to provide similar benefits for individuals who provide homes for their dependents. By making some simple changes we could eliminate the confusion and abuse potential of the Head of Household status while still providing benefits for tax families headed by only one employable adult, a group for which I expect the Head of Household status was originally established.

Concurrent with elimination of the Head of Household status I would increase the exemption for dependents (only) by $1000 per dependent. The current exemption dollar amounts for taxpayers would stay the same. Thus a single taxpayer with two children (for the 2014 tax year) would have combined deductions and exemptions of $6200 + $3950 + $4950 + $4950 = $20050. The same numbers would also hold for an individual whose filing status is 'Married Filing Separately'. This revision provides benefits similar to the deductions for the current Head of Household tax law which provides a combined exemption and deduction of $20,950 ($9100 + $3950 + $3950 + $3950 = $20,950). Note that the revised approach provides slightly less for a single taxpayer with two children. It would be significantly less if there was only one dependent and it would be greater if there were 3 or more dependents. Since household expenses inevitably rise with the number of dependents (more food, more beds, more utilities, increased home size, etc.) I think this revised approach is actually superior to the original in meeting the objective of providing support where support is needed. It also eliminates the unfairness for some filers that I noted in an earlier chapter and removes the perverse financial incentive which currently assesses lower taxes for people living alone than for households shared by more than one taxpayer. I don't think our tax policy should hinder multiple families who want to share living quarters and household expenses. In fact since such arrangements can provide better social support in addition to lower household costs for citizens who desire such home sharing, we should, if anything, encourage such arrangements. Married individuals with dependents who file as 'Married Filing Jointly' would also benefit from the revision because of the increase in the exemption amount for each of their dependents. On the revenue side, this proposal would be approximately neutral for single individuals with dependents but would provide somewhat less tax revenue to the IRS from Married Filing Jointly taxpayers with dependents.

Health Care and the Affordable Care Act (ACA): When thinking about the problems that VITA volunteers have with the ACA, and thinking about the problems that the ACA causes for our clients, it seems to me that we (as a country and a society) have three general types of options. For Option One, we could follow the advice of many vocal people and simply repeal the entire ACA law, returning to the prior state of (in my opinion) health care dysfunction. I don't personally like this Option One, which is a return to a failing system. The costs of doing nothing to improve health care are just too high, both financially and socially.

For Option Two, we would retain the current ACA system and learn to live with it, making tweaks and improvements. Unfortunately, as I've described in Chapter 7, I can't think of any tweaks which would make either the exemption or subsidy issues any better. If we are going to have health care exemptions and premium tax credits, there is no way to determine them correctly until tax filing time of the following year. If we have to live with Option Two, I'm sure that taxpayers will gradually become more familiar with the ACA and that tax preparers will have better training and get more experience over time which will make things a bit easier. Growing familiarity with a complex system, however, does not remove the complexity; the basic problem is the fact that under ACA as currently implemented we will always have exemptions and subsidies. The only way to really fix this issue is to get rid of both exemptions and subsidies.

Thus I prefer an Option Three, which implements a significant fix to the ACA. Option Three would totally remove ACA health care exemptions and subsidy calculations from the tax return preparation process. While Option One (dump the ACA law) would also remove those calculations I believe that health improvement and cost effectiveness is needed and it can be provide by Option Three. A significant reduction in tax program complexity, while increasing effectivity and efficiency, could be obtained through dramatic changes to our provisions for health care. Please stay with me while I described a better approach and give some reasons why change is needed.

The ACA as currently implemented is providing some benefits but at substantial complexity and cost. For some things to work effectively you can't straddle the fence. For some things you can't stay in the middle between public and private delivery. I think basic medical care is one of those things. With the advent of the ACA we are now stuck in an awkward, ineffective, and inefficient middle ground. Our predominantly private health care system, before the ACA, was dysfunctional for those it covered and failed to provide coverage for many. Evidence of the problems before ACA are abundant. Author Steven Brill, as an example, had a major feature article on health care published nationwide in Time Magazine describing why medical bills are so high. His article *'Bitter Pill: Why Medical Bills Are Killing Us'* won a National Magazine Award. The ACA has helped, but did not address all of the problems identified in that article and is causing its own problems. As stated above, some of those problems could be simplified or solved by changing our perspective on how health care should be provided and funded. Rather than being stuck in an awkward, ineffective, and inefficient middle ground I think we should move to single payer health care.

There: I said it. I support Single Payer Health Care. I've 'outed myself'. I've said it even though I know that a great many people in this country strongly oppose that approach to health care and have a visceral negative reaction whenever they even hear the words. To individuals who have that reaction, I hope that you will continue to read as I provide rationale supporting my opinion. Unless we can find another way to make medical care available and affordable, we need to move away from the middle ground and go all the way to 'Single Payer Health Care'. Although I agree that we shouldn't look to big government to solve all our problems, remember that my primary philosophy is that I want programs that we value as a country to be delivered efficiently and effectively in the long term. With that philosophy in mind I don't want to exclude, in an offhand manner, consideration of any approaches that might meet those goals. If, after reading the remainder of this chapter you still don't agree with my approach, then I would hope that you will not stop with just a statement of "No, I don't agree". I don't mind the disagreement, but I'd like you to go further. If not Single Payer, then What? The status quo isn't working. If not Single Payer Option 3, then What?

Let's start a national conversation about ways to actually make things better. As I considered the implications of a single payer approach I found more and more benefits and have gradually become a believer. Let me recap some important items.

The ACA is complex to administer and manage as described in the Chapter 7. Those complexities manifest themselves at tax time mainly in the areas of exemptions and health care premium subsidies. While some exemptions can be obtained early in the year of coverage from the ACA marketplace, others cannot be determined until the year is complete. Exemptions which are dependent on total year income obviously cannot be determined until the year is over. The correct level of health care insurance premium subsidies also cannot be determined until the year is over. With Single Payer Health Care, which does not have exemptions or subsidies, we could completely eliminate these complexities (and make life better for VITA volunteers and our clients.)

As stated in Chapter 7,medical treatment for basic health is not a luxury item. Taxpayers need health care to keep their lives together. As a society we need taxpayers to be healthy to prevent them from becoming a drag on our society. Every individual who we can keep productive is an individual that society as a whole does not need to help support.

Moving beyond the ACA, I further contend that the predominantly employer provided health care system in our country today has outlived its usefulness. Companies need to focus their attention and resources on their primary business products and services. They should focus on what they do best. Concerns about health care divert employer attention, cost them money, and lock in their work forces (which could be considered good or bad). Health care concerns are an unnecessary distraction.

Although the many points made previously are important, I think the point about medical care not being a luxury is the most important and has convinced me that our implementation of the good things in the Affordable Care Act is seriously flawed and needs to be changed. Referring back to earlier chapters, I'd like you to recall that I was very surprised about the reaction of our VITA clients to the ACA. I had anticipated that the response from individuals who did not have health care coverage through employers would be uniformly positive about the ACA. I believed they would be positive because, perhaps for the first time, they would have regular medical care that was affordable. No more need to wait for hours in the emergency room for treatment. No more concerns about normal medical bills and no more qualms of conscience because they were running up medical bills which they knew they would not be able to pay.

Our client's responses were actually quite different. Nearly all are upset that they are being forced to buy something which they don't want and for which they are required to pay penalties if they do not purchase. No one likes to be backed into a corner. Apparently they are used to the situation as it existed and resent having to pay penalties for something that they seem to be already getting at low cost or for nothing. On the other hand, if we move to single payer health plans I do not think that the typical VITA client will be much happier. The clients will still need to make contributions to the health care system and they still won't be happy. Change is hard. However, our current tax system is already set up to reduce the tax burden on lower income people and it would be easy to craft a health care funding approach which is affordable for low income people.

Although many VITA clients apparently don't see the benefit, as a middle class taxpayer I still believe that overall costs for health care in this country would be less if everyone had preventive care and routine health care. I therefore see a benefit to me personally and to society as a whole.

Before I discuss benefits further, I want to define more precisely what I mean when I talk about Single Payer Health Care. Things that I <u>do</u> mean with Single Payer Health care are:

I do mean that while we would all pay as a society, individuals would no longer need to directly pay, or pay an insurance company to pay, for normal care. We should think of such payments as being similar to the Federal Insurance Contributions Act (FICA) taxes that we currently pay during our working years for Medicare insurance and the premiums for Medicare Parts A and B (Hospital and Medical) that are taken from our Social Security payments once we retire. In fact a good way to implement the single payer approach might be to simply expand Medicare (and FICA) so that it covers all citizens, not just the elderly and incapacitated. Why invent a new system when a suitable framework already exists? In fact, we should consider also combining the new system with the current Medicaid system, which provides health coverage to eligible low-income adults, children, pregnant women, elderly adults and people with disabilities. Some have raised the counter argument that we don't want to add additional coverage requirements to Medicare, Medicaid and Social Security programs which are already underfunded and will, unless action is taken, run out of money forcing drastic changes to current coverage. While those concerns are warranted, they aren't relevant since a single payer approach will reduce total costs. The solution to the concerns about Medicare, Medicaid, and Social Security solvency is to fix those programs by either (or both) reducing benefits or raising taxes. The addition of single payer health care would make those solutions easier, not harder.

Basic medical care would, in effect, become a <u>right</u> of every U.S. citizen. And yes, this will cost some money, however the cost avoidance due to reduced complexity along with the increased productivity of our citizenry will more than compensate for single payer health care.

We should also note that FICA already funds some health care services which would be <u>reduced</u> under the proposed single payer approach. To clarify, FICA not only funds Social Security and Medicare but also provides funds to the health care system for institutions that provide healthcare for workers that do not have health insurance and cannot afford healthcare treatment. To the extent that such care will now be provided under the single payer model, current FICA moneys could just be retargeted. Single payer health care would also replace care that is now provided, not by the federal government, but by hospitals, doctors, and other providers using local funding. Expenses for such local charity care are passed on through higher rates for other patients or through local community taxes if those expenses are not ameliorated by state or federal grants and cost sharing programs. Accordingly local health care costs and attendant taxes should also go down and thus would help to offset the rise in FICA taxes.

There are also things that I do <u>not</u> mean when I talk about Single Payer Health Care. I <u>don't</u> mean the following:

I don't mean that the government provides <u>all</u> health care. It should only provide preventative, basic, and routine health care, as currently generally defined by the ACA.

Cosmetic surgeries, most elective surgeries, and cutting edge health care would be still funded by individuals and provided via private insurance companies and medical providers.

I don't mean that the government would necessarily directly provide the above basic health care. The manner in which medical services would be provided will need to be determined. One simple implementation would be to simply extend the current Medicare coverage approach to everyone of all ages. Two other approaches currently in broad usage in this country are the Veterans Administration (VA) approach and the TANF approach. When comparing those three approaches, Medicare reimburses private physicians, in contrast VA facilities, doctors and staff are largely direct government employees, while TANF takes yet a third approach for care delivery. TANF largely hires contractors to provide medical staff and treatment. The merits of all three approaches should be compared, but any of the three could be applied in combination with a Single Payer system.

I don't mean that all health insurance companies will go out of business. We are only talking about basic care. Even original Medicare does not provide full coverage and there are many insurance companies who sell people 'Medigap' plans of various predefined tiers which provide additional coverage for additional cost. Our current 'free market' medical service model will still exist, it just won't need to cover basic care.

With those definitions and elaborations in mind, let me discuss some specifics related to the cost versus benefit equation for single payer health care. In the following paragraphs, I will discuss how that approach would change the low and middle income taxpayer's approach to life, and how it could beneficially change other aspects of the tax code.

I want to start with the topic of individual ethics. As a society, we are moving away from the bad old days of what we used to call 'the welfare society'. Instead we place more importance on provisions such the Earned Income Credit, which only provides aid to individuals who are earning income. Part of the rationale for that change has been that there is a stigma associated with needing to rely upon others. Especially when individuals cannot get out of that cycle of being helped, they lose self-esteem and lose the motivation to be self-supporting. Unconscious mental processes such as "I'm not good enough to support myself, no matter how hard I try, so why should I try?" become ingrained in that individual and that segment of society. Thoughts like that can then lead to another layer of dysfunction with thoughts like "It's not my fault that I can't support myself. I'm as good as anyone else. It is the system, and injustices done to me (or my culture, or my ancestors, or my language, or any of many other excuses [pick one or a few]) that is keeping me down. They owe me support because it isn't my fault.". Single Payer health care helps to prevent that cycle of negative thought. If basic health care is available to everyone, not just to me but for everyone, the stigma associated with not being able to afford medical care is removed.

Improvement of citizen's mental perspective is important, but the real dollar costs are also important. If basic medical care is provided, individuals are more likely to enjoy better preventive care, which will keep them healthy and employable. Further, preventive care will reduce the expense of the more intensive and expensive medical care needed to correct problems that could have been caught earlier. If people and their children are healthier they are less likely to be absent from their jobs. For less serious health problems, if preventive care keeps them from suffering from minor maladies they will be more productive in their employment. If they do a better job because of the above, they are more likely to stay employed or to advance to even better positions.

Individuals who are healthier and who won't get swamped by medical bills for routine or urgent care are less likely to suffer from the 'one crises away' syndrome. That syndrome occurs when people are living 'on the edge' of solvency. They could be knocked off by just one crisis: a medical emergency, an eviction, a job loss. They don't have enough money to weather a financial storm that lasts 90 days. They have a job, are making ends meet, but then there is an injury, there is an illness, their child needs help, etc. Whatever the crises, people on the edge can fall into destitution and homelessness as the result of just one crises. Individuals who fall off the edge into insolvency become a drain on society and on other social programs. Having free preventive and routine medical care removes one of the major causes for that condition.

Please note that I said previously that basic health care should be provided for everyone. Not just lower income, not just college educated, not just any other group but rather every citizen of the country. That is why I think that the current employer based health care model (which is diminishing but still prevalent in our country) also needs to change. You might ask, why change employer based health care, which is a system that works?

While I agree that employer based health care has worked, and I've personally benefited from it during my working career, I think its time has passed. Society is more fluid. Efficiency in companies is more important than it has ever been. With only a few exceptions, health care is not the primary concern nor in the product line of most companies. Companies in the past provided health care as a recruitment and retention aid. There was no other reasonable alternative available for their prospective employees. That is no longer as true. Health care costs have risen so rapidly that companies are trying their best to limit and outsource their medical costs for employees and retirees. I am a direct witness to this trend because my former employer has just notified all retirees that we are being transitioned (with some remaining company financial support) to the commercial insurance industry. While this is a bit personally unsettling I understand why they are shedding that non-essential service.

95

My personal example supports my contention that the health care world for employees of large companies is already shifting.

Universal single payer health care will be beneficial for employees for several reasons. Availability of health coverage for them and their families will no longer hinder them from changing from one employer to another, allowing them to better match their interests and skills with the needs of employers. Having a more ideal fit between employers and employees should lead to more engaged, committed and productive employees, benefiting their employers and the entire economy.

A primary benefit of single payer plans should be lower overall health care costs. Study after study comparing costs and health outcomes of the US approach in comparison with countries which have single payer systems shows that our current costs are much higher while our health outcomes are no better. The fact that costs are lower for single payer plans makes complete sense to me simply when considering the overhead involved in our current approach. The paperwork and administrative costs are tremendous. As individuals, we can each think about the number of forms that we've had to fill out, the agony of having to decide which insurance plan is best, based on confusing summaries of benefits and then, once a selection has been made, the mind numbing pages of 'Evidence of Coverage' documentation that describe what is covered and to what percentage after copays and deductibles. Then add to that the time we've spent in the doctor's office talking with the intake staff who handle benefit paperwork. They are not medical people, they are clerical people solely employed to manage insurance coverage. Add to that the additional effort by the health care professionals themselves trying to determine which services are covered and are 'in network' for individuals who have elected network based health coverage. For basic care, single payer coverage can nearly eliminate all of those costs.

Since the focus of this book is income tax preparation for VITA clients, I want to spend a paragraph moving back from the general health care topic and talking about how Single Payer Health care would affect the current tax preparation process. Simply stated, ACA premium tax credits would no longer be necessary and ACA health coverage exemptions would not be necessary. Almost all the paperwork associated with the ACA would just disappear because it all relates to funding, rather than to care for health. From the perspective of a taxpayer (or a VITA volunteer) it would be wonderful! If the funding for Single Payer health care requires payments from individuals, those payments could be easily incorporated into the existing tax system simply by reducing the standard values for exemptions or deductions. Since every citizen would be covered in the same way, the new deduction and exemption values would require no additional computations. Changes to deductions or exemptions would also automatically shield very low income taxpayers from a health care obligation because if their deductions and exemptions were larger than their income, they would not have any health care payments, in the same way that many now don't pay any taxes.

A movement to Single Payer Health Care would appear to have little impact on the need for the existing Earned Income Credit and Child Tax Credit. There is a decent probability, however, that the amount of those payments could be reduced if basic health care, and the costs of that health care, were removed as a concern from the taxpayer.

Recapping my comments about health care, I want to summarize my proposed changes to health care in this country via a brief comparison of three health care approaches, as those approaches apply to the VITA client population. Those three are 1) Health Care Before the ACA, 2) Health Care as currently Implemented via the ACA, and 3) My proposed Single Payer approach to ACA.

Health Care Before the ACA: For those without employer provided health care and without individual insurance, health care relied on hope; hope that no one got injured or sick. Preventive care was absent. When medical care was needed it was provided by one-time encounters with the medical establishment, frequently via hospital emergency room visits. The resulting bills either burdened the taxpayer with debt or were subsidized or 'written off' as charity care by hospitals and medical professionals. The provided charity care in turn raised either health care costs and/or taxes for the rest of us.

Health Care via the ACA: For those eligible for the ACA, and who can afford the subsidized insurance premiums, preventive care is provided at no cost, other than their insurance premiums. Needed medical care is provided at reduced costs with better defined deductibles and co-pays. For hospitals and doctors, the costs of providing charity care are lower. However, the ACA system is complex and requires the forcing function of penalties to ensure high rates of participation. Overall costs should be reduced because of preventive care, but overhead costs have increased.

Single Payer ACA Implementation: The benefits of ACA still remain, but the overhead cost and complexity of administration would be removed.

Chapter Nine: Summary

Part One of this book was intended to give prospective VITA volunteers and other interested readers a factual description of the Volunteer Income Tax Assistance program with insights, anecdotes, and dilemmas drawn from the author's experience as a tax preparer for low to moderate income individuals. I hope that my experiences give prospective VITA volunteers a feeling about what to expect as they begin their own service to the taxpaying community.

Part Two provided some history about certain aspects of the tax code and my perceptions about why they were implemented. We need to understand that history in order to form a basis for the improvement suggestions provided later in Part Two. My initial comments were motivated by VITA experiences, but I'm sure that you've noted that my recommendations have moved far from that more limited scope. I hope that readers find my comments thought provoking. Perhaps if more of us understand the involved issues and discuss possible solutions, we can influence our elected legislators to implement changes that would be good for both individuals and for our society. If some or many readers disagree with my analysis and solutions, I am still happy. I doubt that any of these ideas are unique or newly described. We need a broader understanding of our taxation approach and our social welfare infrastructure to develop a consensus approach to which we can all subscribe. Let us not 'Just Say No' to improvement. If there are better ways to improve, let's talk about them and recommend them.

Glossary

In an attempt to assist readers who find that acronyms are a problem, I am providing the following condensed definitions.

ACA: Affordable Care Act. This abbreviation is actually a shortened form of the full title of the 2010 health care law which is the **Patient Protection and Affordable Care Act.** The ACA is also informally known as Obamacare.

AGI: Adjusted Gross Income. Taxable income of tax filers prior to subtraction of deductions and exemptions.

CTC: Child Tax Credit, A non-refundable credit which may be supplemented in certain circumstances by the separate and refundable 'Additional Child Tax Credit'.

EIC: Earned Income Credit, formerly known as the EITC.

EITC: Earned Income Tax Credit, has been renamed EIC.

Form 1095-A: Health Insurance Marketplace Statement for ACA.

Form 1095-B: Health Coverage Statement for ACA.

Form 1095-C: Employer-Provided Health Insurance Offer and Coverage Insurance for ACA.

Form 1098-T: A Tuition Statement provided to students by their education institutions to document tuition payments and scholarship amounts.

Form 1099-MISC: IRS form used by employers to report Miscellaneous Income payments to employees and contractors. With 'box 7' checked, this form documents Non-Employee Compensation.

Form 8962: IRS Form used to calculate and report ACA Premium Tax Credit.

Form 8965: IRS Form used to determine and report ACA Health Coverage Exemptions.

IRS: Internal Revenue Service.

ITIN: Individual Taxpayer Identification Number. Although Social Security numbers are also ITINs, in this book ITIN normally refers to non-US-citizens who need an identification number to pay taxes or access benefits.

Josie: My big black Labrador Retriever who missed me while I was volunteering to help people with taxes.

MEC: Minimum Essential Coverage as required by the Affordable Care Act.

MFJ: Married Filing Jointly.

ODWIN: 'Opening Doors for Women in Need', the VITA site in Fort Worth, Texas where I volunteered.

Pub 4012: IRS Publication 4012: VITA/TCE Volunteer Resource Guide.

QSR: The Quality Site Requirements which are part of the VITA Volunteer Standards of Conduct.

SNAP: Supplemental Nutrition Assistance Program. Formerly known as Food Stamps.

SPEC: the Stakeholder Partnerships, Education and Communication function of the IRS.

TANF: Temporary Assistance for Needy Families.

TCE: Tax Counseling for the Elderly.

VITA: Volunteer Income Tax Assistance.

VSC: the VITA Volunteer Standards of Conduct.

W2: An IRS form used by employers to record and document income earned by their employees as a result of their employment.

WIC: Women, Infants, and Children. A welfare program supporting women, infants and children.

Bibliography and References

1. Information on VITA from IRS Web Site and from the IRS regulations covering VITA and SPEC in the Internal Revenue Manual Part 22 at www.irs.gov/irm/part22/irm_22-030-001.html

2. VITA beginnings (Excerpts from Gary Iskowitz in the Journal of Accountancy) from http://www.journalofaccountancy.com/Issues/2010/Sep/LastWord.htm and http://www.isko.com/

3. The Economic Policy Institute report located at URL http://www.epi.org/publication/ib370-earned-income-tax-credit-and-the-child-tax-credit-history-purpose-goals-and-effectiveness/

About The Author

Larry Klos is a retired engineering manager who decided to share stories of his life, experiences, and imaginings with a broader public. He has been writing both professionally and as an avocation for many years. Larry grew up on a farm in rural Montana and his wife Elaine grew up in a row home in Philadelphia. Despite disparate backgrounds they have a common value system and, with two children, six grandchildren and a series of dogs, have lived and volunteered in Texas for more than 40 years. Works produced to date include both fiction and nonfiction books.

ALSO BY   LARRY KLOS

The Klos Family House: A Memoir
Our Dog Neighbors
Life, Death, and Airplanes: A Memoir
Stories with Twists

www.ingramcontent.com/pod-product-compliance
Lightning Source LLC
Chambersburg PA
CBHW070821180526
45168CB00002B/704